Defoe Abbott Marx Hardy Machiavelli Haggard Chesterton Emerson Joyce Austen Hugo Eliot Grimm

Melville Montaigne Cooper Molière

Stoker Carroll Christie Maupassant Byron Schiller

Wilde Garnett Engels Smith Kafka

Goethe Einstein Fitzgerald Hawthorne Hall

Cotton Dostoyevsky Willis

Baum Henry Kipling Doyle

Leslie Dumas Flaubert Turgenev Nietzsche Balzac

Stockton Vatsyayana Crane

Burroughs Verne

Curtis Tocqueville Gogol Vinci

Homer Widger Tolstoy Whitman Busch

Darwin Thoreau Twain

Potter Freud Zola Lawrence Plato Scott Harte

Kant Jowett Stevenson Dickens Burton Hesse

Andersen

London Descartes Cervantes Voltaire

Poe Aristotle Wells Cooke

Hale James Hastings Burton

Bunner Shakespeare Irving

Richter Chekhov da Shaw Benedict Alcott

Doré Dante Swift Chambers Wodehouse Pushkin Newton

tredition®

tredition was established in 2006 by Sandra Latusseck and Soenke Schulz. Based in Hamburg, Germany, tredition offers publishing solutions to authors and publishing houses, combined with world-wide distribution of printed and digital book content. tredition is uniquely positioned to enable authors and publishing houses to create books on their own terms and without conventional manu-facturing risks.

For more information please visit: www.tredition.com

TREDITION CLASSICS

This book is part of the TREDITION CLASSICS series. The creators of this series are united by passion for literature and driven by the intention of making all public domain books available in printed format again - worldwide. Most TREDITION CLASSICS titles have been out of print and off the bookstore shelves for decades. At tredition we believe that a great book never goes out of style and that its value is eternal. Several mostly non-profit literature projects provide content to tredition. To support their good work, tredition donates a portion of the proceeds from each sold copy. As a reader of a TREDITION CLASSICS book, you support our mission to save many of the amazing works of world literature from oblivion. See all available books at www.tredition.com.

Project Gutenberg

The content for this book has been graciously provided by Project Gutenberg. Project Gutenberg is a non-profit organization founded by Michael Hart in 1971 at the University of Illinois. The mission of Project Gutenberg is simple: To encourage the creation and distribution of eBooks. Project Gutenberg is the first and largest collection of public domain eBooks.

The Christmas Kalends of Provence And Some Other Provençal Festivals

Thomas A. (Thomas Allibone) Janvier

Imprint

This book is part of TREDITION CLASSICS

Author: Thomas A. (Thomas Allibone) Janvier
Cover design: Buchgut, Berlin – Germany

Publisher: tredition GmbH, Hamburg - Germany
ISBN: 978-3-8472-3407-4

www.tredition.com
www.tredition.de

Copyright:
The content of this book is sourced from the public domain.

The intention of the TREDITION CLASSICS series is to make world literature in the public domain available in printed format. Literary enthusiasts and organizations, such as Project Gutenberg, worldwide have scanned and digitally edited the original texts. tredition has subsequently formatted and redesigned the content into a modern reading layout. Therefore, we cannot guarantee the exact reproduction of the original format of a particular historic edition. Please also note that no modifications have been made to the spelling, therefore it may differ from the orthography used today.

The
Christmas Kalends
of
Provence

Thomas A.
Janvier

[See p. 32

"'TO THE HEALTH OF THE COUNT!'"

ILLUSTRATED

TO

C. A. J.

Contents

Illustrations

The Christmas Kalends
of Provence

I

Fancy you've journeyed down the Rhône,
Fancy you've passed Vienne, Valence,
Fancy you've skirted Avignon—
And so are come *en pleine* Provence.

Fancy a mistral cutting keen
Across the sunlit wintry fields,
Fancy brown vines, and olives green,
And blustered, swaying, cypress shields.

Fancy a widely opened door,
Fancy an eager outstretched hand,
Fancy—nor need you ask for more—
A heart-sped welcome to our land.

Fancy the peal of Christmas chimes,
Fancy that some long-buried year
Is born again of ancient times—
And in Provence take Christmas cheer!

In my own case, this journey and this welcome were not fancies but realities. I had come to keep Christmas with my old friend Monsieur de Vièlmur according to the tradi [4] tional Provençal rites and ceremonies in his own entirely Provençal home: an ancient dwelling which stands high up on the westward slope of the Alpilles, overlooking Arles and Tarascon and within sight of Avignon, near the Rhône margin of Provence.

The Vidame—such is Monsieur de Vièlmur's ancient title: dating from the vigorous days when every proper bishop, himself not averse to taking a breather with sword and battle-axe should fighting matters become serious, had his *vice dominus* to lead his forces in the field — is an old-school country gentleman who is amiably at odds with modern times. While tolerant of those who have yielded to the new order, he himself is a great stickler for the preservation of antique forms and ceremonies: sometimes, indeed, pushing his fancies to lengths that fairly would lay him open to the charge of whimsicality, were not even the most extravagant of his crotchets touched and mellowed by his natural goodness of heart. In the earlier stages of our acquaintance I was disposed to regard him as an eccentric; but a wider knowledge of Provençal matters [5] has convinced me that he is a type. Under his genial guidance it has been my privilege to see much of the inner life of the Provençaux, and his explanations have enabled me to understand what I have seen: the Vidame being of an antiquarian and bookish temper, and never better pleased than when I set him to rummaging in his memory or his library for the information which I require to make clear to me some curious phase of Provençal manners or ways.

The Château de Vièlmur has remained so intimately a part of the Middle Ages that the subtle essence of that romantic period still pervades it, and gives to all that goes on there a quaintly archaic tone. The donjon, a prodigiously strong square tower dating from the twelfth century, partly is surrounded by a dwelling in the florid style of two hundred years back — the architectural flippancies of which have been so tousled by time and weather as to give it the look of an old beau caught unawares by age and grizzled in the midst of his affected youth.

In the rear of these oddly coupled struct [6] ures is a farm-house with a dependent rambling collection of farm-buildings; the whole enclosing a large open court to which access is had by a vaulted passage-way, that on occasion may be closed by a double set of ancient iron-clamped doors. As the few exterior windows of the farm-house are grated heavily, and as from each of the rear corners of the square there projects a crusty tourelle from which a raking fire could be kept up along the walls, the place has quite the air of a testy little fortress — and a fortress it was meant to be when it was built three hundred years and more ago (the date, 1561, is carved on the keystone of the arched entrance) in the time of the religious wars.

But now the iron-clamped doors stand open on rusty hinges, and the court-yard has that look of placid cheerfulness which goes with the varied peaceful activities of farm labour and farm life. Chickens and ducks wander about it chattering complacently, an aged goat of a melancholy humour stands usually in one corner lost in misanthropic thought, and a great flock of extraordinarily tame pigeons flutters back and forth between the [7] stone dove-cote rising in a square tower above the farm-house and the farm well.

AT THE WELL

This well — enclosed in a stone well-house surmounted by a very ancient crucifix — is in the centre of the court-yard, and it also is the centre of a little domestic world. To its kerb come the farm animals three times daily; while as frequently, though less regularly, most of the members of the two households come there too; and there do the humans—notably, I have observed, if they be of different sexes—find it convenient to rest for a while together and take a dish of friendly talk. From the low-toned chattering and the soft laughter that I have heard now and then of an evening I have inferred that these nominally chance encounters are not confined wholly to the day.

By simple machinery (of which the motive-power is an aged patient horse, who is started and left then to his own devices; and who works quite honestly, save that now and then he stops in his round and indulges himself in a little doze) the well-water is raised continuously into a long stone trough. Thence the overflow is led away to irrigate the garden [8] of the Château: an old-fashioned garden, on a slope declining southward and westward, abounding in balustraded terraces and stone benches stiffly ornate, and having here and there stone nymphs and goddesses over which in summer climbing roses kindly (and discreetly) throw a blushing veil.

The dependent estate is a large one: lying partly on the flanks of the Alpilles, and extending far outward from the base of the range over the level region where the Rhône valley widens and merges into the valley of the Durance. On its highest slopes are straggling rows of almond trees, which in the early spring time belt the grey mountains with a broad girdle of delicate pink blossoms; a little lower are terraced olive-orchards, a pale shimmering green the year round—the olive continuously casting and renewing its leaves; and the lowest level, the wide fertile plain, is given over to vineyards and wheat-fields and fields of vegetables (grown for the Paris market), broken by plantations of fruit-trees and by the long lines of green-black cypress which run due east and west across the landscape and shield the tender [9] growing things from the north wind, the mistral.

The Château stands, as I have said, well up on the mountain-side; and on the very spot (I must observe that I am here quoting its owner) where was the camp in which Marius lay with his legions until the time was ripe for him to strike the blow that secured

Southern Gaul to Rome. This matter of Marius is a ticklish subject to touch on with the Vidame: since the fact must be admitted that other antiquaries are not less firm in their convictions, nor less hot in presenting them, that the camp of the Roman general was variously elsewhere—and all of them, I regret to add, display a lamentable acerbity of temper in scouting each other's views. Indeed, the subject is of so irritating a complexion that the mere mention of it almost surely will throw my old friend—who in matters not antiquarian has a sweetness of nature rarely equalled—into a veritable fuming rage.

But even the antiquaries are agreed that, long before the coming of the Romans, many earlier races successively made on this moun [10] tain promontory overlooking the Rhône delta their fortified home: for here, as on scores of other defensible heights throughout Provence, the merest scratching of the soil brings to light flints and potshards which tell of varied human occupancy in very far back times. And the antiquaries still farther are agreed that precisely as these material relics (only a little hidden beneath the present surface of the soil) tell of diverse ancient dwellers here, so do the surviving fragments of creeds and customs (only a little hidden beneath the surface of Provençal daily life) tell in a more sublimate fashion of those same vanished races which marched on into Eternity in the shadowy morning of Time.

For this is an old land, where many peoples have lived their spans out and gone onward—yet have not passed utterly away. Far down in the popular heart remnants of the beliefs and of the habits of those ancients survive, entranced: yet not so numbed but that, on occasion, they may be aroused into a life that still in part is real. Even now, when the touch-stone is applied—when the thrilling of some nerve of memory or of instinct brings [11] the present into close association with the past—there will flash into view still quick particles of seemingly long-dead creeds or customs rooted in a deep antiquity: the faiths and usages which of old were cherished by the Kelto-Ligurians, Phœnicians, Grecians, Romans, Goths, Saracens, whose blood and whose beliefs are blended in the Christian race which inhabits Provence to-day.

II

In the dominion of Vièlmur there is an inner empire. Nominally, the Vidame is the reigning sovereign; but the power behind his throne is Misè Fougueiroun. The term "Misè" is an old-fashioned Provençal title of respect for women of the little bourgeoisie — tradesmen's and shopkeepers' wives and the like — that has become obsolescent since the Revolution and very generally has given place to the fine-ladyish "Madamo." With a little stretching, it may be rendered by our English old-fashioned title of "mistress"; and Misè Fougueiroun, who is the Vidame's [12] housekeeper, is mistress over his household in a truly masterful way.

This personage is a little round woman, still plumply pleasing although she is rising sixty, who is arrayed always with an exquisite neatness in the dress — the sober black-and-white of the elder women, not the gay colours worn by the young girls — of the Pays d'Arles; and — although shortness and plumpness are at odds with majesty of deportment — she has, at least, the peremptory manner of one long accustomed to command. As is apt to be the way with little round women, her temper is of a brittle cast and her hasty rulings sometimes smack of injustice; but her nature (and this also is characteristic of her type) is so warmly generous that her heart easily can be caught into kindness on the rebound. The Vidame, who in spite of his antiquarian testiness is something of a philosopher, takes advantage of her peculiarities to compass such of his wishes as happen to run counter to her laws. His Machiavellian policy is to draw her fire by a demand of an extravagant nature; and then, when her lively refusal has set her a little in the wrong, hand [13] somely to ask of her as a favour what he really requires — a method that never fails of success.

By my obviously sincere admiration of the Château and its surroundings, and by a discreet word or two implying a more personal admiration — a tribute which no woman of the Pays d'Arles ever is too old to accept graciously — I was so fortunate as to win Misè Fougueiroun's favour at the outset; a fact of which I was apprised on the evening of my arrival — it was at dinner, and the housekeeper herself had brought in a bottle of precious Châteauneuf-du-Pape — by the cordiality with which she joined forces with the Vidame in reprobating my belated coming to the Château. Actually, I was near a fortnight behind the time named in my invitation: which had stated expressly that Christmas began in Provence on the Feast of Saint Barbara, and that I was expected not later than that day — December 4th.

"Monsieur should have been here," said the housekeeper with decision, "when we planted the blessed Saint Barbara's grain. And now it is grown a full span. Monsieur will not see Christmas at all!" [14]

But my apologetic explanation that I never even had heard of Saint Barbara's grain only made my case the more deplorable.

"Mai!" exclaimed Misè Fougueiroun, in the tone of one who faces suddenly a real calamity. "Can it be that there are no Christians in monsieur's America? Is it possible that down there they do not keep the Christmas feast at all?"

To cover my confusion, the Vidame intervened with an explanation which made America appear in a light less heathenish. "The planting of Saint Barbara's grain," he said, "is a custom that I think is peculiar to the South of France. In almost every household in Provence, and over in Languedoc too, on Saint Barbara's day the women fill two, sometimes three, plates with wheat or lentils which they set afloat in water and then stand in the warm ashes of the fire-place or on a sunny window ledge to germinate. This is done in order to foretell the harvest of the coming year, for as Saint Barbara's grain grows well or ill so will the harvest of the coming year be good or bad; and also that there may be on the table when the Great [15] Supper is served on Christmas Eve — that is to say, on the feast of the Winter Solstice — green growing grain in symbol or in earnest of the harvest of the new year that then begins.

PLANTING

SAINT BARBARA'S GRAIN

"The association of the Trinitarian Saint Barbara with this custom," the Vidame continued, "I fear is a bit of a makeshift. Were three plates of grain the rule, something of a case would be made out in her favour. But the rule, so far as one can be found, is for only two. The custom must be of Pagan origin, and therefore dates from far back of the time when Saint Barbara lived in her three-windowed tower at Heliopolis. Probably her name was tagged to it because of old these votive and prophetic grain-fields were sown on

20

what in Christian times became her dedicated day. But whatever light-mannered goddess may have been their patroness then, she is their patroness now; and from their sowing we date the beginning of our Christmas feast."

It was obvious that this explanation of the custom went much too far for Misè Fougueiroun. At the mention of its foundation in Paganism she sniffed audibly, and upon the [16] Vidame's reference to the light-mannered goddess she drew her ample skirts primly about her and left the room.

The Vidame smiled. "I have scandalized Misè, and to-morrow I shall have to listen to a lecture," he said, and in a moment continued: "It is not easy to make our Provençaux realize how closely we are linked to older peoples and to older times. The very name for Christmas in Provençal, Calèndo, tells how this Christian festival lives on from the Roman festival of the Winter Solstice, the January Kalends; and the beliefs and customs which go with its celebration still more plainly mark its origin. Our farmers believe, for instance, that these days which now are passing—the twelve days, called *coumtié*, immediately preceding Christmas—are foretellers of the weather for the new twelve months to come; each in its turn, by rain or sunshine or by heat or cold, showing the character of the correspondingly numbered month of the new year. That the twelve prophetic days are those which immediately precede the solstice puts their endowment with prophetic power very far back into antiquity. Our farmers, [17] too, have the saying, 'When Christmas falls on a Friday you may sow in ashes'—meaning that the harvest of the ensuing year surely will be so bountiful that seed sown anywhere will grow; and in this saying there is a strong trace of Venus worship, for Friday—Divèndre in Provençal—is the day sacred to the goddess of fertility and bears her name. That belief comes to us from the time when the statue of Aphrodite, dug up not long since at Marseille, was worshipped here. Our *Pater de Calèndo*—our curious Christmas prayer for abundance during the coming year—clearly is a Pagan supplication that in part has been diverted into Christian ways; and in like manner comes to us from Paganism the whole of our yule-log ceremonial."

The Vidame rose from the table. "Our coffee will be served in the library," he said. He spoke with a perceptible hesitation, and there was anxiety in his tone as he added: "Misè makes superb coffee; but sometimes, when I have offended her, it is not good at all." And he visibly fidgeted until the coffee arrived, and proved by its excellence that the housekeeper had been too noble to take revenge. [18]

III

In the early morning a lively clatter rising from the farm-yard came through my open window, along with the sunshine and the crisp freshness of the morning air. My apartment was in the south-east angle of the Château, and my bedroom windows—overlooking the inner court—commanded the view along the range of the Alpilles to the Luberoun and Mont-Ventour, a pale great opal afloat in waves of clouds; while from the windows of my sitting-room I saw over Mont-Majour and Arles far across the level Camargue to the hazy horizon below which lay the Mediterrænean.

In the court-yard there was more than the ordinary morning commotion of farm life, and the buzz of talk going on at the well and the racing and shouting of a parcel of children all had in it a touch of eagerness and expectancy. While I still was drinking my coffee—in the excellence and delicate service of which I recognized the friendly hand [19] of Misè Fougueiroun—there came a knock at my door; and, upon my answer, the Vidame entered—looking so elate and wearing so blithe an air that he easily might have been mistaken for a frolicsome middle-aged sunbeam.

"Hurry! Hurry!" he cried, while still shaking both my hands. "This is a day of days—we are going now to bring home the *cacho-fiò*, the yule-log! Put on a pair of heavy shoes—the walking is rough on the mountain-side. But be quick, and come down the moment that you are ready. Now I must be off. There is a world for me to do!" And the old gentleman bustled out of the room while he still was speaking, and in a few moments I heard him giving orders to some one with great animation on the terrace below.

When I went down stairs, five minutes later, I found him standing in the hall by the open doorway: through which I saw, bright in the morning light across the level landscape, King René's castle and the church of Sainte-Marthe in Tarascon; and over beyond Tarascon, high on the farther bank of the Rhône, [20] Count Raymond's castle of Beaucaire; and in the far distance, faintly, the jagged peaks of the Cévennes.

But that was no time for looking at landscapes. "Come along!" he cried. "They all are waiting for us at the Mazet," and he hurried me down the steps to the terrace and so around to the rear of the Château, talking away eagerly as we walked.

"It is a most important matter," he said, "this bringing home of the *cacho-fiò*. The whole family must take part in it. The head of the family—the grandfather, the father, or the eldest son—must cut the tree; all the others must share in carrying home the log that is to make the Christmas fire. And the tree must be a fruit-bearing tree. With us it usually is an almond or an olive. The olive especially is sacred. Our people, getting their faith from their Greek ancestors, believe that lightning never strikes it. But an apple-tree or a pear-tree will serve the purpose, and up in the Alp region they burn the acorn-bearing oak. What we shall do to-day is an echo of Druidical ceremonial—of the time when the Druid priests cut the yule-oak and with their [21] golden sickles reaped the sacred mistletoe; but old Jan here, who is so stiff for preserving ancient customs, does not know that this custom, like many others that he stands for, is the survival of a rite."

While the Vidame was speaking we had turned from the terrace and were nearing the Mazet—which diminutive of the Provençal word *mas*, meaning farm-house, is applied to the farm establishment at Vièlmur partly in friendliness and partly in indication of its dependence upon the great house, the Château. At the arched entrance we found the farm family awaiting us: Old Jan, the steward of the estate, and his wife Elizo; Marius, their elder son, a man over forty, who is the active manager of affairs; their younger son, Esperit, and their daughter Nanoun; and the wife of Marius, Janetoun, to whose skirts a small child was clinging while three or four larger children scampered about her in a whir of excitement over the imminent event by which Christmas really would be ushered in.

When my presentation had been accomplished—a matter a little complicated in the [22] case of old Jan, who, in common with most of the old men hereabouts, speaks only Provençal—we set off across the home vineyard, and thence went upward through the olive-orchards, to the high region on the mountain-side where grew the almond-tree which the Vidame and his steward in counsel together had selected for the Christmas sacrifice.

Nanoun, a strapping red-cheeked black-haired bounce of twenty, ran back into the Mazet as we started; and joined us again, while we were crossing the vineyard, bringing with her a gentle-faced fair girl of her own age who came shyly. The Vidame, calling her Magali, had a cordial word for this new-comer; and nudged me to bid me mark how promptly Esperit was by her side. "It is as good as settled," he whispered. "They have been lovers since they were children. Magali is the daughter of Elizo's foster-sister, who died when the child was born. Then Elizo brought her home to the Mazet, and there she has lived her whole lifelong. Esperit is waiting only until he shall be established in the world to speak the word. And the scamp is in a hurry. Actually, he [23] is pestering me to put him at the head of the Lower Farm!"

The Vidame gave this last piece of information in a tone of severity; but there was a twinkle in his kind old eyes as he spoke which led me to infer that Master Esperit's chances for the stewardship of the Lower Farm were anything but desperate, and I noticed that from time to time he cast very friendly glances toward these young lovers—as our little procession, mounting the successive terraces, went through the olive-orchards along the hill-side upward.

Presently we were grouped around the devoted almond-tree: a gnarled old personage, of a great age and girth, having that pathetic look of sorrowful dignity which I find always in superannuated trees—and now and then in humans of gentle natures who are conscious that their days of usefulness are gone. Esperit, who was beside me, felt called upon to explain that the old tree was almost past bearing and so was worthless. His explanation seemed to me a bit of needless cruelty; and I was glad when Magali, evidently moved by the same feeling, intervened softly with: [24] "Hush, the poor tree may understand!" And then added, aloud: "The old almond must know that it is a very great honour for any tree to be chosen for the Christmas fire!"

This little touch of pure poetry charmed me. But I was not surprised by it—for pure poetry, both in thought and in expression, is found often among the peasants of Provence.

Even the children were quiet as old Jan took his place beside the tree, and there was a touch of solemnity in his manner as he swung his heavy axe and gave the first strong blow—that sent a shiver through all the branches, as though the tree realized that death had overtaken it at last. When he had slashed a dozen times into the trunk, making a deep gash in the pale red wood beneath the brown bark, he handed the axe to Marius; and stood watching silently with the rest of us while his son finished the work that he had begun. In a few minutes the tree tottered; and then fell with a growling death-cry, as its brittle old branches crashed upon the ground.

Whatever there had been of unconscious reverence in the silence that attended the felling was at an end. As the tree came down [25] everybody shouted. Instantly the children were swarming all over it. In a moment our little company burst into the flood of loud and lively talk that is inseparable in Provence from gay occasions—and that is ill held in check even at funerals and in church. They are the merriest people in the world, the Provençaux.

IV

Marius completed his work by cutting through the trunk again, making a noble *cacho-fiò* near five feet long—big enough to burn, according to the Provençal rule, from Christmas Eve until the evening of New Year's Day.

It is not expected, of course, that the log shall burn continuously. Each night it is smothered in ashes and is not set a-blazing again until the following evening. But even when thus husbanded the log must be a big one to last the week out, and it is only in rich households that the rule can be observed. Persons of modest means are satisfied if they [26] can keep burning the sacred fire over Christmas Day; and as to the very poor, their *cacho-fiò* is no more than a bit of a fruit-tree's branch—that barely, by cautious guarding, will burn until the midnight of Christmas Eve. Yet this suffices: and it seems to me that there is something very tenderly touching about these thin yule-twigs which make, with all the loving ceremonial and rejoicing that might go with a whole tree-trunk, the poor man's

Christmas fire. In the country, the poorest man is sure of his *cacho-fiò*. The Provençaux are a kindly race, and the well-to-do farmers are not forgetful of their poorer neighbors at Christmas time. An almond-branch always may be had for the asking; and often, along with other friendly gifts toward the feast, without any asking at all. Indeed, as I understood from the Vidame's orders, the remainder of our old almond was to be cut up and distributed over the estate and about the neighborhood — and so the life went out from it finally in a Christmas blaze that brightened many homes. In the cities, of course, the case is different; and, no doubt, on many a chill hearth no yule-fire burns. [27] But even in the cities this kindly usage is not unknown. Among the boat-builders and ship-wrights of the coast towns the custom long has obtained — being in force even in the Government dock-yard at Toulon — of permitting each workman to carry away a *cacho-fiò* from the refuse oak timber; and an equivalent present frequently is given at Christmas time to the labourers in other trades.

While the Vidame talked to me of these genial matters we were returning homeward, moving in a mildly triumphal procession that I felt to be a little tinctured with ceremonial practices come down from forgotten times. Old Jan and Marius marching in front, Esperit and the sturdy Nanoun marching behind, carried between them the yule-log slung to shoulder-poles. Immediately in their wake, as chief rejoicers, the Vidame and I walked arm in arm. Behind us came Elizo and Janetoun and Magali — save that the last (manifesting a most needless solicitude for Nanoun, who almost could have carried the log alone on her own strapping shoulders) managed to be frequently near Esperit's side. The children, waving olive-branches, career [28] ed about us; now and then going through the form of helping to carry the *cacho-fiò*, and all the while shouting and singing and dancing — after the fashion of small dryads who also were partly imps of joy. So we came down through the sun-swept, terraced olive-orchards in a spirit of rejoicing that had its beginning very far back in the world's history and yet was freshly new that day.

Our procession took on grand proportions, I should explain, because our yule-log was of extraordinary size. But always the yule-log is brought home in triumph. If it is small, it is carried on the shoulder of the father or the eldest son; if it is a goodly size, those two carry it together; or a young husband and wife may bear it between them—as we actually saw a thick branch of our almond borne away that afternoon—while the children caracole around them or lend little helping hands.

Being come to the Mazet, the log was stood on end in the court-yard in readiness to be taken thence to the fire-place on Christmas Eve. I fancied that the men handled it with a certain reverence; and the Vidame assured me that such actually was the case. Already, [29] being dedicate to the Christmas rite, it had become in a way sacred; and along with its sanctity, according to the popular belief, it had acquired a power which enabled it sharply to resent anything that smacked of sacrilegious affront. The belief was well rooted, he added by way of instance, that any one who sat on a yule-log would pay in his person for his temerity either with a dreadful stomach-ache that would not permit him to eat his Christmas dinner, or would suffer a pest of boils. He confessed that he always had wished to test practically this superstition, but that his faith in it had been too strong to suffer him to make the trial!

On the other hand, when treated reverently and burned with fit-ting rites, the yule-log brings upon all the household a blessing; and when it has been consumed even its ashes are potent for good. In-fused into a much-esteemed country-side medicine, the yule-log ashes add to its efficacy; sprinkled in the chicken-house and cow-stable, they ward off disease; and, being set in the linen-closet, they are an infallible protection against fire. Probably this last property has its genesis in the [30] belief that live-coals from the yule-log may be placed on the linen cloth spread for the Great Supper without setting it on fire—a belief which prudent housewives always are shy of putting to a practical test.

The home-bringing ceremony being thus ended, we walked back to the Château together—startling Esperit and Magali standing hand in hand, lover-like, in the archway; and when we were come to the terrace, and were seated snugly in a sunny corner, the Vid-ame told me of a very stately yule-log gift that was made anciently in Aix—and very likely elsewhere also—in feudal times.

In Aix it was the custom, when the Counts of Provence still lived and ruled there, for the magistrates of the city each year at Christmas-tide to carry in solemn procession a huge *cacho-fiò* to the palace of their sovereign; and there formally to present to him — or, in his absence, to the Grand Seneschal on his behalf — this their free-will and good-will offering. And when the ceremony of presentation was ended the city fathers were served with a collation at the Count's charges, and [31] were given the opportunity to pledge him loyally in his own good wine.

Knowing Aix well, I was able to fill in the outlines of the Vidame's bare statement of fact and also to give it a background. What a joy the procession must have been to see! The grey-bearded magistrates, in their velvet caps and robes, wearing their golden chains of office; the great log, swung to shoulder-poles and borne by leathern-jerkined henchmen; surely drummers and fifers, for such a ceremonial would have been impossibly incomplete in Provence without a *tambourin* and *galoubet*; doubtless a brace of ceremonial trumpeters; and a seemly guard in front and rear of steel-capped and steel-jacketed halbardiers. All these marching gallantly through the narrow, yet stately, Aix streets; with comfortable burghers and well-rounded matrons in the doorways looking on, and pretty faces peeping from upper windows and going all a-blushing because of the over-bold glances of the men-at-arms! And then fancy the presentation in the great hall of the castle; and the gay feasting; and the merry wagging of grey-bearded chins as the [32] magistrates cried all together, "To the health of the Count!" — and tossed their wine!

I protest that I grew quite melancholy as I thought how delightful it all was — and how utterly impossible it all is in these our own dull times! In truth I never can dwell upon such genially picturesque doings of the past without feeling that Fate treated me very shabbily in not making me one of my own ancestors — and so setting me back in that hard-fighting, gay-going, and eminently light-opera age.

V

As Christmas Day drew near I observed that Misè Fougueiroun walked thoughtfully and seemed to be oppressed by heavy cares. When I met her on the stairs or about the passages her eyes had the far-off look of eyes prying into a portentous future; and when I spoke to her she recovered her wandering wits with a start. At first I feared that some grave misfortune had overtaken her; but I was reassured, upon applying [33] myself to the Vidame, by finding that her seeming melancholy distraction was due solely to the concentration of all her faculties upon the preparation of the Christmas feast.

Her case, he added, was not singular. It was the same just then with all the housewives of the region: for the chief ceremonial event of Christmas in Provence is the *Gros Soupa* that is eaten upon Christmas Eve, and of even greater culinary importance is the dinner that is eaten upon Christmas Day — wherefore does every woman brood and labour that her achievement of those meals may realize her high ideal! Especially does the preparation of the Great Supper compel exhaustive thought. Being of a vigil, the supper necessarily is "lean"; and custom has fixed unalterably the principal dishes of which it must be composed. Thus limited straitly, the making of it becomes a struggle of genius against material conditions; and its successful accomplishment is comparable with the perfect presentment by a great poet of some well-worn elemental truth in a sonnet — of which the triumphant beauty comes less from the integral concept than from the ex [34] quisite felicity of expression that gives freshness to a hackneyed subject treated in accordance with severely constraining rules.

It is no wonder, therefore, that the Provençal housewives give the shortest of the December days to soulful creation in the kitchen, and the longest of the December nights to searching for inspired culinary guidance in dreams. They take such things very seriously, those good women: nor is their seriousness to be wondered at when we reflect that Saint Martha, of blessed memory, ended her days here in Provence; and that this notable saint, after delivering the country from the ravaging Tarasque, no doubt set up in her own house at Tarascon an ideal standard of housekeeping that still is in force. Certainly, the women of this region pattern themselves so closely upon their sainted model as to be even more cumbered with much serving than are womenkind elsewhere.

Because of the Vidame's desolate bachelorhood, the kindly custom long ago was established that he and all his household every year should eat their Great Supper with the [35] farm family at the Mazet; an arrangement that did not work well until Misè Fougueiroun and Elizo (after some years of spirited squabbling) came to the agreement that the former should be permitted to prepare the delicate sweets served for dessert at that repast. Of these the most important is nougat, without which Christmas would be as barren in Provence as Christmas would be in England without plum-pudding or in America without mince-pies. Besides being sold in great quantities by town confectioners, nougat is made in most country homes. Even the dwellers on the poor up-land farms — which, being above the reach of irrigation, yield uncertain harvests — have their own almond-trees and their own bees to make them honey, and so possess the raw materials of this necessary luxury. As for the other sweets, they may be anything that fancy and skill together can achieve; and it is in this ornate department of the Great Supper that genius has its largest chance.

But it was the making of the Christmas dinner that mainly occupied Misè Fougueiroun's mind — a feast pure and simple, gov [36] erned by the one jolly law that it shall be the very best dinner of the whole year! What may be termed its by-laws are that the principal dish shall be a roast turkey, and that nougat and *poumpo* shall figure at the dessert. Why *poumpo* is held in high esteem by the Provençaux I am not prepared to say. It seemed to me a cake of only a humdrum quality; but even Misè Fougueiroun — to whom I am indebted for the appended recipe [1] — spoke of it in a sincerely admiring and chop-smacking way.

Anciently the Christmas bird was a goose — who was roasted and eaten ('twas a backhanded compliment!) in honour of her ancestral good deeds. For legend tells that when the Kings, led by the star, arrived at the inn-stable in Bethlehem it was the goose, alone of all the animals assembled there, who came forward politely to make them her [37] compliments; yet failed to express clearly her good intentions because she had caught a cold, in the chill and windy weather, and her voice was unintelligibly creaky and harsh. The same voice ever since has remained to her, and as a farther commemoration of her hospitable and courteous conduct it became the custom to spit her piously on Christmas Day.

I have come across the record of another Christmas roast that now and then was served at the tables of the rich in Provence in mediæval times. This was a huge cock, stuffed with chicken-livers and sausage-meat and garnished with twelve roasted partridges, thirty eggs, and thirty truffles: the whole making an alimentary allegory in which the cock represented the year, the partridges the months, the eggs the days, and the truffles the nights. But this never was a common dish, and not until the turkey appeared was the goose rescued from her annual martyrdom.

The date of the coming of the turkey to Provence is uncertain. Popular tradition declares that the crusaders brought him home [38] with them from the Indies! Certainly, he came a long while ago; probably very soon after Europe received him from America as a noble and perpetual Christmas present—and that occurred, I think, about thirty years after Columbus, with an admirable gastronomic perception, discovered his primitive home.

Ordinarily the Provençal Christmas turkey is roasted with a stuffing of chestnuts, or of sausage-meat and black olives: but the high cooks of Provence also roast him stuffed with truffles—making so superb a dish that Brillat-Savarin has singled it out for praise. Misè Fougueiroun's method, still more exquisite, was to make a stuffing of veal and fillet of pork (one-third of the former and two-thirds of the latter) minced and brayed in a mortar with a seasoning of salt and pepper and herbs, to which truffles cut in quarters were added with a lavish hand. For the basting she used a piece of salt-pork fat stuck on a long fork and set on fire. From this the flaming juice was dripped judiciously over the roast, with resulting little puffings of brown skin which permitted the savour of the salt to penetrate the flesh and so gave to it a delicious [39] crispness and succulence. As to the flavour of a turkey thus cooked, no tongue can tell what any tongue blessed to taste of it may know! Of the minor dishes served at the Christmas dinner it is needless to speak. There is nothing ceremonial about them; nothing remarkable except their excellence and their profusion. Save that they are daintier, they are much the same as Christmas dishes in other lands.

While the preparation of all these things was forward, a veritable culinary tornado raged in the lower regions of the Château. Both

Magali and the buxom Nanoun were summoned to serve under the housekeeper's banners, and I was told that they esteemed as a high privilege their opportunity thus to penetrate into the very arcana of high culinary art. The Vidame even said that Nanoun's matrimonial chances—already good, for the baggage had set half the lads of the country-side at loggerheads about her—would be decidedly bettered by this discipline under Misè Fougueiroun: whose name long has been one to conjure with in all the kitchens between Saint-Remy and the Rhône. For the [40] Provençaux are famous trencher-men, and the way that leads through their gullets is not the longest way to their hearts.

VI

But in spite of their eager natural love for all good things eatable, the Provençaux also are poets; and, along with the cooking, another matter was in train that was wholly of a poetic cast. This was the making of the crèche: a representation with odd little figures and accessories of the personages and scene of the Nativity—the whole at once so naïve and so tender as to be possible only among a people blessed with rare sweetness and rare simplicity of soul.

The making of the crèche is especially the children's part of the festival—though the elders always take a most lively interest in it— and a couple of days before Christmas, as we were returning from one of our walks, we fell in with all the farm children coming homeward from the mountains laden with crèche-making material: mosses, lichens, laurel, and [41] holly; this last of smaller growth than our holly, but bearing fine red berries, which in Provençal are called *li poumeto de Sant-Jan*—"the little apples of Saint John."

Our expedition had been one of the many that the Vidame took me upon in order that he might expound his geographical reasons for believing in his beloved Roman Camp; and this diversion enabled me to escape from Marius—I fear with a somewhat unseemly precipitation—by pressing him for information in regard to the matter which the children had in hand. As to openly checking the Vidame, when once he fairly is astride of his hobby, the case is hopeless. To cast a doubt upon even the least of his declarations touching the doings of the Roman General is the signal for a blaze of arguments down all his battle front; and I really do not like even to speculate upon what might happen were I to meet one of his major propositions with a flat denial! But an attack in flank, I find—the sudden posing of a question upon some minor antiquarian theme— usually can be counted upon, as in this instance, to draw him outside the Roman lines. Yet that he [42] left them with a pained reluctance was so evident that I could not but feel some twinges of remorse—until my interest in what he told me made me forget my heartlessness in shunting to a side track the subject on which he so loves to talk.

In a way, the crèche takes in Provence the place of the Christmas-tree, of which Northern institution nothing is known here; but it is closer to the heart of Christmas than the tree, being touched with a little of the tender beauty of the event which it represents in so quaint a guise. Its invention is ascribed to Saint Francis of Assisi. The chronicle of his Order tells that this seraphic man, having first obtained the permission of the Holy See, represented the principal scenes of the Nativity in a stable; and that in the stable so transformed he celebrated mass and preached to the people. All this is wholly in keeping with the character of Saint Francis; and, certainly, the crèche had its origin in Italy in his period, and in the same conditions which formed his graciously fanciful soul. Its introduction into Provence is said to have been in the time of John XXII.—the second of the Avignon [43] Popes, who came to the Pontificate in the year 1316—and by the Fathers of the Oratory of Marseille: from which centre it rapidly spread abroad through the land until it became a necessary feature of the Christmas festival both in churches and in homes.

Obviously, the crèche is an offshoot from the miracle plays and mysteries which had their beginning a full two centuries earlier. These also survive vigorously in Provence in the "Pastouralo": an acted representation of the Nativity that is given each year during the Christmas season by amateurs or professionals in every city and town, and in almost every village. Indeed, the Pastouralo is so large a subject, and so curious and so interesting, that I venture here only to allude to it. Nor has it, properly—although so intensely a part of the Provençal Christmas—a place in this paper, which especially deals with the Christmas of the home.

In the farm-houses, and in the dwellings of the middle-class, the crèche is placed always in the living-room, and so becomes an intimate part of the family life. On a table set in a corner is represented a rocky hill-side [44] — dusted with flour to represent snow — rising in terraces tufted with moss and grass and little trees and broken by foot-paths and a winding road. This structure is very like a Provençal hill-side, but it is supposed to represent the rocky region around Bethlehem. At its base, on the left, embowered in laurel or in holly, is a wooden or pasteboard representation of the inn; and beside the inn is the stable: an open shed in which are grouped little figures representing the several personages of the Nativity. In the centre is the Christ-Child, either in a cradle or lying on a truss of straw; seated beside him is the Virgin; Saint Joseph stands near, holding in his hand the mystic lily; with their heads bent down over the Child are the ox and the ass — for those good animals helped with their breath through that cold night to keep him warm. In the foreground are the two *ravi* — a man and a woman in awed ecstasy, with upraised arms — and the adoring shepherds. To these are added on Epiphany the figures of the Magi — the Kings, as they are called always in French and in Provençal — with their train of attendants, and the cam [45] els on which they have brought their gifts. Angels (pendent from the farm-house ceiling) float in the air above the stable. Higher is the Star, from which a ray (a golden thread) descends to the Christ-Child's hand. Over all, in a glory of clouds, hangs the figure of Jehovah attended by a white dove.

These are the essentials of the crèche; and in the beginning, no doubt, these made the whole of it. But for nearly six centuries the delicate imagination of the Provençal poets and the cruder, but still poetic, fancy of the Provençal people have been enlarging upon the simple original: with the result that twoscore or more figures often are found in the crèche of to-day.

Either drawing from the quaintly beautiful mediæval legends of the birth and childhood of Jesus, or directly from their own quaintly simple souls, the poets from early times have been making Christmas songs — noëls, or nouvé as they are called in Provençal — in which new subordinate characters have been created in a spirit of frank realism, and these have materialized in new figures surrounding the crèche. At the same time the fancy of [46] the people, working with a still more naïve directness along the lines of associated ideas, has been making the most curiously incongruous and anachronistic additions to the group.

To the first order belong such creations as the blind man, led by a child, coming to be healed of his blindness by the Infant's touch; or that of the young mother hurrying to offer her breast to the new-born (in accordance with the beautiful custom still in force in Provence) that its own mother may rest a little before she begins to suckle it; or that of the other mother bringing the cradle of which her own baby has been dispossessed, because of her compassion for the poor woman at the inn whose child is lying on a truss of straw.

But the popular additions, begotten of association of ideas, are far more numerous and also are far more curious. The hill-top, close under the floating figure of Jehovah, has been crowned with a wind-mill—because wind-mills abounded anciently on the hill-tops of Provence. To the mill, naturally, has been added a miller—who is riding down the road on an ass, with a sack of flour across his [47] saddle-bow that he is carrying as a gift to the Holy Family. The adoring shepherds have been given flocks of sheep, and on the hill-side more shepherds and more sheep have been put for company. The sheep, in association with the ox and the ass, have brought in their train a whole troop of domestic animals—including geese and turkeys and chickens and a cock on the roof of the stable; and in the train of the camels has come the extraordinary addition of lions, bears, leopards, elephants, ostriches, and even crocodiles! The Provençaux being from of old mighty hunters (the tradition has found its classic embodiment in Tartarin), and hill-sides being appropriate to hunting, a figure of a fowler with a gun at his shoulder has been introduced; and as it is well, even in the case of a Provençal sports-man, to point a gun at a definite object, the fowler usually is so placed as to aim at the cock on the stable roof. He is a modern, yet not very recent addition, the fowler, as is shown by the fact that he carries a flint-lock fowling-piece. Drumming and fifing being absolute essentials to every sort of Provençal festivity, a conspicuous figure [48] always is found playing on a *tambourin* and *galoubet*. Itinerant knife-grinders are an old institution here, and in some obscure way—possibly because of their thievish propensities—are associated intimately with the devil; and so there is either a knife-grinder simple, or a devil with a knife-grinder's wheel. Of old it was the custom for the women to carry distaffs and to spin out thread as they went to and from the fields or along the roads (just as the women nowadays knit as they walk), and therefore a spinning-woman always is of the company. Because child-stealing was not uncommon here formerly, and because gypsies still are plentiful, there are three gypsies lurking about the inn all ready to steal the Christ-Child away. As the inn-keeper naturally would come out to investigate the cause of the commotion in his stable-yard, he is found, with the others, lantern in hand. And, finally, there is a group of women bearing as gifts to the Christ-Child the essentials of the Christmas feast: codfish, chickens, carde, ropes of garlic, eggs, and the great Christmas cakes, *poumpo* and *fougasso*.

Many other figures may be, and often are, [49] added to the group—of which one of the most delightful is the Turk who makes a solacing present of his pipe to Saint Joseph; but all of these which I have named have come to be now quite as necessary to a properly made crèche as are the few which are taken direct from the Bible narrative: and the congregation surely is one of the quaintest that ever poetry and simplicity together devised!

In Provençal the diminutive of saint is *santoun*; and it is as santouns that all the personages of the crèche—including the whole of the purely human and animal contingent, and even the knife-grinding devil—are known. They are of various sizes—the largest, used in churches, being from two to three feet high—and in quality of all degrees: ranging downward from real magnificence (such as may be seen in the seventeenth-century Neapolitan crèche in Room V. of the Musée de Cluny) to the rough little clay figures two or three inches high in common household use throughout Provence. These last, sold by thousands at Christmas time, are as crude as they well can be: pressed in rude moulds, dried (not baked), and painted with glaring [50] colours, with a little gilding added in the case of Jehovah and the angels and the Kings.

For two centuries or more the making of clay santouns has been a notable industry in Marseille. It is largely a hereditary trade carried on by certain families inhabiting that ancient part of the city, the Quarter of Saint-Jean, which lies to the south of the Vieux Port. The

figures sell for the merest trifle, the cheapest for one or two sous, yet
the Santoun Fair — held annually in December in booths set up in
the Cour-du-Chapitre and in the Allée-des-Capucins — is of a real
commercial importance; and is also — what with the oddly whimsical nature of its merchandise, and the vast enjoyment of the children
under parental or grand-parental convoy who are its patrons — the
very gayest sight in that city of which gayety is the dominant characteristic the whole year round.

VII

Not until "the day of the Kings," the Feast of the Epiphany, is the
crèche completed. Then are added to the group [51] the figures of
the three Kings — the Magi, as we call them in English: along with
their gallant train of servitors, and the hump-backed camels on
which they have ridden westward to Bethlehem guided by the Star.
The Provençal children believe that they come at sunset, in pomp
and splendour, riding in from the outer country, and on through the
street of the village, and in through the church door, to do homage
before the manger in the transept where the Christ-Child lies. And
the children believe that it may be seen, this noble procession, if
only they may have the good fortune to hit upon the road along
which the royal progress to their village is to be made. But Mistral
has told about all this far better than I can tell about it, and I shall
quote here, by his permission, a page or two from the "Memoirs"
which he is writing, slowly and lovingly, in the between-whiles of
the making of his songs:

"To-morrow's the festival of the Kings. This evening they arrive. If
you want to see them, little ones, go quickly to meet them — and
take presents for them, and for their [52] pages, and for the poor
camels who have come so far!"

That was what, in my time, the mothers used to say on the eve of
Epiphany — and, *zòu!* all the children of the village would be off
together to meet "les Rois Mages," who were coming with their
pages and their camels and the whole of their glittering royal suite
to adore the Christ-Child in our church in Maillane! All of us together, little chaps with curly hair, pretty little girls, our sabots
clacking, off we would go along the Arles road, our hearts thrilling
with joy, our eyes full of visions. In our hands we would carry, as

we had been bidden, our presents: fougasso for the Kings, figs for the pages, sweet hay for the tired camels who had come so far.

On we would go through the cold of dying day, the sun, over beyond the Rhône, dipping toward the Cévennes; leafless trees, red in low sun-rays; black lines of cypress; in the fields an old woman with a fagot on her head; beside the road an old man scratching under the hedge for snails.

"Where are you going, little ones?"

"We are going to meet the Kings!" And [53] on we would run proudly along the white road, while the shrewd north wind blew sharp behind us, until our old church tower would drop away and be hidden behind the trees. We could see far, far down the wide straight road, but it would be bare! In the cold of the winter evening all would be dumb. Then we would meet a shepherd, wrapped in his long brown cloak and leaning on his staff, a silhouette against the western sky.

"Where are you going, little ones?"

"We are going to meet the Kings! Can you tell us if they are far off?"

"Ah, the Kings. Certainly. They are over there behind the cypresses. They are coming. You will see them soon."

On we would run to meet the Kings so near, with our fougasso and our figs and our hay for the hungry camels. The day would be waning rapidly, the sun dropping down into a great cloud-bank above the mountains, the wind nipping us more shrewdly as it grew still more chill. Our hearts also would be chilling. Even the bravest of us would be doubting a little this adventure upon which we were bound. [54]

THE PASSING OF THE KINGS

Then, of a sudden, a flood of radiant glory would be about us, and from the dark cloud above the mountains would burst forth a splendour of glowing crimson and of royal purple and of glittering gold!

"Les Rois Mages! Les Rois Mages!" we would cry. "They are coming! They are here at last!"

But it would be only the last rich dazzle of the sunset. Presently it would vanish. The owls would be hooting. The chill night would be settling down upon us, out there in the bleak country, sorrowful, alone. Fear would take hold of us. To keep up our courage a little, we would nibble at the figs which we had hoped to give to the pages, at the fougasso which we had hoped to present to the Kings. As for the hay for the hungry camels, we would throw it away. Shivering in the wintry dusk, we would return sadly to our homes.

And when we reached our homes again our mothers would ask: "Well, did you see them, the Kings?"

"No; they passed by on the other side of the Rhône, behind the mountains." [55]

"But what road did you take?"

"The road to Arles."

"Ah, my poor child! The Kings don't come that way. They come from the East. You should have gone out to meet them on the road to Saint-Remy. And what a sight you have missed! Oh, how beautiful it was when they came marching into Maillane—the drums, the trumpets, the pages, the camels! *Mon Dieu*, what a commotion! What a sight it was! And now they are in the church, making their homage before the manger in which the little Christ-Child lies. But never mind; after supper you shall see them all."

Then we would sup quickly, and so be off to the church, crowded with all Maillane. Barely would we be entered there when the organ would begin, at first softly and then bursting forth formidably, all our people singing with it, with the superb noël:

> In the early morning
> I met a train
> Of three great Kings who were going on a journey!

High up before the altar, directly above the manger in which the Christ-Child was [56] lying, would be the glittering *bello estello*; and making their homage before the manger would be the Kings whom it had guided thither from the East: old white-bearded King Melchior with his gift of incense; gallant young King Gaspard with his gift of treasure; black King Balthazar the Moor with his gift of myrrh. How reverently we would gaze on them, and how we would admire the brave pages who carried the trains of their long mantles, and the hump-backed camels whose heads towered high above Saint Mary and Saint Joseph and the ox and the ass.

Yes, there they were at last — the Kings!

Many and many a time in the after years have I gone a-walking on the Arles road at nightfall on the Eve of the Kings. It is the same — but not the same. The sun, over beyond the Rhône, is dipping toward the Cévennes; the leafless trees are red in the low sunrays; across the fields stretch the black lines of cypress; even the old man, as long ago, is scratching in the hedge by the roadside for snails. And when darkness [57] comes quickly, with the sun's setting, the owls hoot as of old.

But in the radiant glory of the sunset I no longer see the dazzle and the splendour of the Kings!

"Which way went they, the Kings?"

"Behind the mountains!"

VIII

In the morning of the day preceding Christmas a lurking, yet ill-repressed, excitement pervaded the Château and all its dependencies. In the case of the Vidame and Misè Fougueiroun the excitement did not even lurk: it blazed forth so openly that they were as a brace of comets — bustling violently through our universe and dragging into their erratic wakes, away from normal orbits, the whole planetary system of the household and all the haply intrusive stars.

With my morning coffee came the explanation of a quite impossible smell of frying dough-nuts which had puzzled me on the pre [58] ceding day: a magnificent golden-brown *fougasso*, so perfect of its kind that any Provençal of that region — though he had come upon it in the sandy wastes of Sahara — would have known that its creator was Misè Fougueiroun. To compare the *fougasso* with our homely dough-nut does it injustice. It is a large flat open-work cake — a grating wrought in dough — an inch or so in thickness, either plain or sweetened or salted, fried delicately in the best olive-oil of Aix or Maussane. It is made throughout the winter, but its making at Christmas time is of obligation; and the custom obtains among the women — though less now than of old — of sending a *fougasso* as a Christmas gift to each of their intimates. As this custom had in it something more than a touch of vainglorious emulation, I well can understand why it has fallen into desuetude in the vicinity of Vièlmur — where Misè Fougueiroun's inspired kitchening throws all other cook-work hopelessly into the shade. As I ate the "horns" (as its fragments are called) of my *fougasso* that morning, dipping them in my coffee according to the [59] prescribed custom, I was satisfied that it deserved its high place in the popular esteem.

When I joined the Vidame below stairs I found him under such stress of Christmas excitement that he actually forgot his usual morning suggestion — made always with an off-hand freshness, as though the matter were entirely new — that we should take a turn along the lines of the Roman Camp. He was fidgeting back and forth between the hall (our usual place of morning meeting) and the kitchen: torn by his conflicting desires to attend upon me, his guest, and to take his accustomed part in the friendly ceremony that was going on below. Presently he compromised the divergencies of the situation, though with some hesitation, by taking me down with him into Misè Fougueiroun's domain — where he became frankly cheerful when he found that I was well received.

Although the morning still was young, work on the estate had been ended for the day, and about the door of the kitchen more than a score of labourers were gathered: all [60] with such gay looks as to show that something of a more than ordinarily joyous nature was in train. Among them I recognized the young fellow whom we had met with his wife carrying away the yule-log; and found that all of them were workmen upon the estate who — either being married or having homes within walking distance — were to be furloughed for the day. This was according to the Provençal custom that Christmas must be spent by one's own fire-side; and it also was according to Provençal custom that they were not suffered to go away with empty hands.

Misè Fougueiroun — a plump embodiment of Benevolence — stood beside a table on which was a great heap of her own *fougasso*, and big baskets filled with dried figs and almonds and celery, and a genial battalion of bottles standing guard over all. One by one the vassals were called up—there was a strong flavour of feudalism in it all—and to each, while the Vidame wished him a *"Bòni fèsto!"* the housekeeper gave his Christmas portion: a *fougasso*, a double-handful each of figs and almonds, a stalk of celery, and a bottle of [61] *vin cue* [2]—the cordial that is used for the libation of the yule-log and for the solemn yule-cup; and each, as he received his portion, made his little speech of friendly thanks—in several cases most gracefully turned—and then was off in a hurry for his home. Most of them were dwellers in the immediate neighbourhood; but four or five had before them walks of more than twenty miles, with the same distance to cover in returning the next day. But great must be the difficulty or the distance that will keep a Provençal [62] from his own people and his own hearth-stone at Christmas-tide!

In illustration of this home-seeking trait, I have from my friend Mistral the story that his own grandfather used to tell regularly every year when all the family was gathered about the yule-fire on Christmas Eve:

It was back in the Revolutionary times, and Mistral the grandfather—only he was not a grandfather then, but a mettlesome young soldier of two-and-twenty—was serving with the Army of the Pyrénées, down on the borders of Spain. December was well on, but the season was open—so open that he found one day a tree still bearing oranges. He filled a basket with the fruit and carried it to the Captain of his company. It was a gift for a king, down there in those hard times, and the Captain's eyes sparkled. "Ask what thou wilt, *mon brave,*" he said, "and if I can give it to thee it shall be thine."

Quick as a flash the young fellow answered: "Before a cannon-ball cuts me in two, Commandant, I should like to go to Provence and help once more to lay the yule-log in my own home. Let me do that!" [63]

Now that was a serious matter. But the Captain had given his word, and the word of a soldier of the Republic was better than the oath of a king. Therefore he sat down at his camp-table and wrote:

Army of the Eastern Pyrénées, December 12, 1793.

We, Perrin, Captain of Military Transport, give leave to the citizen François Mistral, a brave Republican soldier, twenty-two years old, five feet six inches high, chestnut hair and eyebrows, ordinary nose, mouth the same, round chin, medium forehead, oval face, to go back into his province, to go all over the Republic, and, if he wants to, to go to the devil!

"With an order like that in his pocket," said Mistral, "you can fancy how my grandfather put the leagues behind him; and how joyfully he reached Maillane on the lovely Christmas Eve, and how there was danger of rib-cracking from the hugging that went on. But the next day it was another matter. News of his coming had flown about the town, and the Mayor sent for him.

"'In the name of the law, citizen,' the Mayor demanded, 'why hast thou left the army?'

"Now my grandfather was a bit of a wag, and so—with never a word about his famous [64] pass—he answered: 'Well, you see I took a fancy to come and spend my Christmas here in Maillane.'

"At that the Mayor was in a towering passion. 'Very good, citizen,' he cried. 'Other people also may take fancies—and mine is that thou shalt explain this fancy of thine before the Military Tribunal at Tarascon. Off with him there!'

"And then away went my grandfather between a brace of gendarmes, who brought him in no time before the District Judge: a savage old fellow in a red cap, with a beard up to his eyes, who glared at him as he asked: 'Citizen, how is it that thou hast deserted thy flag?'

"Now my grandfather, who was a sensible man, knew that a joke might be carried too far; therefore he whipped out his pass and presented it, and so in a moment set everything right.

"'Good, very good, citizen!' said old Redcap. 'This is as it should be. Thy Captain says that thou art a brave soldier of the Republic, and that is the best that the best of us can be. With a pass like that in thy pocket [65] thou canst snap thy fingers at all the mayors in Provence; and the devil himself had best be careful—shouldst thou go down that way, as thy pass permits thee—how he trifles with a brave soldier of France!'

"But my grandfather did not try the devil's temper," Mistral con-
cluded. "He was satisfied to stay in his own dear home until the
Day of the Kings was over, and then he went back to his command."

IX

The day dragged a little when we had finished in the kitchen with
the giving of Christmas portions and the last of the farm-hands,
calling back "*Bòni fèsto!*," had gone away. For the womenkind, of
course, there was a world to do; and Misè Fougueiroun whisked us
out of her dominions with a pretty plain statement that our company was less desirable than our room. But for the men there was only
idle waiting until night should come.

As for the Vidame—who is a fiery fume of [66] a little old gentleman, never happy unless in some way busily employed—this period of stagnation was so galling that in sheer pity I mounted him
upon his hobby and set him to galloping away. 'Twas an easy matter, and the stimulant that I administered was rather dangerously
strong: for I brought up the blackest beast in the whole herd of his
abominations by asking him if there were not some colour of reason
in the belief that Marius lay not at Vièlmur but at Glanum—now
Saint-Remy-de-Provence—behind the lines of Roman wall which
exist there to this day.

So far as relieving the strain of the situation was concerned, my
expedient was a complete success; but the storm that I raised was
like to have given the Vidame such an attack of bilious indigestion
begotten of anger as would have spoiled the Great Supper for him;
and as for myself, I was overwhelmed for some hours by his ava-
lanche of words. But the long walk that we took in the afternoon,
that he might give me convincing proof of the soundness of his
archæological theories, fortunately set matters right again; [67] and
when we returned in the late day to the Château my old friend had
recovered his normal serenity of soul.

As we passed the Mazet in our afternoon walk, we stopped to
greet the new arrivals there, come to make the family gathering
complete: two more married children, with a flock of their own little
ones, and Elizo's father and mother—a bowed little rosy-cheeked
old woman and a bowed lean old man, both well above eighty
years. There was a lively passage of friendly greetings between

them all and the Vidame; and it was quite delightful to see how the bowed little old woman kindled and bridled when the Vidame gallantly protested that she grew younger and handsomer every year.

A tall ladder stood against the Mazet, and the children were engaged in hanging tiny wheat-sheaves along the eaves: the Christmas portion of the birds. In old times, the Vidame explained, it was the general custom for children to make this pretty offering—that the birds of heaven, finding themselves so served, might descend in clouds to the feast prepared for them by Christian [68] bounty. But nowadays, he added, sighing, the custom rarely was observed.

Other charitable usages of Christmas had vanished, he continued, because the need for them had passed away with the coming of better times. Save in the large cities, there are very few really poor people in Provence now. It is a rich land, and it gives to its hard-working inhabitants a good living; with only a pinch now and then when a cold winter or a dry summer or a wet harvest puts things out of gear. But of old the conditions were sadly different and there was need for all that charity could give.

In those times, when in comfortable homes the Christmas feast was set, there would be heard outside a plaintive voice calling: "Give something from your yule-log to the sorrowful poor!" And then the children quickly, would carry out to the calling poor one good portions of food. Pious families, also, were wont to ask some poor friend or acquaintance, or even a poor passing stranger, to eat the Great Supper with them; and of the fragments a part would be sent to the poor brethren in the Hostel de Dieu: which offerings [69] were called always "the share of the good God."

In many towns and villages the offerings of Christian bounty were collected in a curious way. A gigantic figure of wicker-work—called Melchior, after one of the three Kings of the Epiphany—clothed in a grotesque fashion and with a huge pannier strapped to his back, was mounted upon an ass and so was taken from door to door to gather for the poor whatever the generous would give of food. Into the big basket charitable hands threw figs, almonds, bread, cheese, olives, sausages: and when the brave Melchior had finished his round his basket was emptied upon a table at the church door, and then all the poor people of the parish were free to come there and receive portions of those good things — while the church bells rang, and while there blazed beside the table a torch in representation of the Star which guided Melchior and his fellow kings to Bethlehem.

A reminiscence of this general charity still survives in the little town of Solliès, tucked away in the mountains not far from Toulon. There, at Christmas time, thirteen poor peo [70] ple known as "the Apostles" (though there is one to spare) receive at the town-house a dole of two pounds of meat, two loaves of bread, some figs and almonds, and a few sous. And throughout Provence the custom still is general that each well-to-do family shall send a portion of its Christmas loaf — the *pan calendau* — to some friend or neighbour to whom Fortune has been less kind. But, happily, this gift nowadays often is a mere friendly compliment, like the gift of *fougasso*; for the times are past when weak-kneed and spasmodic charity dealt with real poverty in Provence.

X

'Twas with such kindly reminiscences of old-time benevolence, rather than with explosive archæological matters, that I kept the Vidame from falling again a-fuming — while we waited through the dusk for the coming of seven o'clock, at which hour the festivities at the Mazet were to begin. Our waiting place was the candle-lit salon: a stately old [71] apartment floored formally with squares of black and white marble, furnished in the formal style of the eighteenth century, and hung around with formal family portraits and curious old prints in which rather lax classical subjects were treated with a formal severity. The library being our usual habitat, I inferred that our change of quarters was in honour of the day. It was much to my liking; for in that antiquely ordered room — and the presence of the Vidame helped the illusion — I felt always as though I had stepped backward into the thick of eighteenth century romance. But for the Vidame, although he also loves its old time flavour, the salon had no charms just then; and when the glass-covered clock on the man- tle chimed from among its gilded cupids the three-quarters he arose with a brisk alacrity and said that it was time for us to be off.

Our march — out through the rear door of the Château and across the court-yard to the Mazet — was processional. All the household

went with us. The Vidame gallantly gave his arm to Misè Fougueiroun; I followed with her first officer—a sauce-box named [72]
Mouneto, so plumply provoking and charming in her Arlesian
dress that I will not say what did or did not happen in the darkness
as we passed the well! A little in our rear followed the house-
servants, even to the least; and in the Mazet already were gathered,
with the family, the few work-people of the estate who had not
gone to their own homes. For the Great Supper is a patriarchal feast,
to which in Christian fellowship come the master and the master's
family and all of their servitors and dependants on equal terms.

A broad stream of light came out through the open doorway of
the farm-house, and with it a great clatter and buzz of talk—that
increased tenfold as we entered, and a cry of *"Bòni fèsto!"* came from
the whole company at once. As for the Vidame, he so radiated cordiality that he seemed to be the veritable Spirit of Christmas (incar-
nate at the age of sixty, and at that period of the nineteenth century
when stocks and frilled shirts were worn), and his joyful old legs
were near to dancing as he went among the company with warm-
hearted greetings and outstretched hands. [73]

All told, we numbered above forty; but the great living-room of
the Mazet, notwithstanding the space taken by the supper-table
ranged down the middle of it, easily could have held another score.
Save in its size, and in the completeness of its appointments, this
room was thoroughly typical of the main apartment found in farm-
houses throughout Provence. The floor was laid with stone slabs
and the ceiling was supported upon very large smoke-browned
beams—from which hung hams, and strings of sausages, and ropes
of garlic, and a half-dozen bladders filled with lard. More than a
third of the rear wall was taken up by the huge fire-place, that
measured ten feet across and seven feet from the stone mantle-shelf
to the floor. In its centre, with room on each side in the chimney-
corners for a chair (a space often occupied by large lockers for flour
and salt), was the fire-bed—crossed by a pair of tall andirons, which
flared out at the top into little iron baskets (often used, with a filling
of live coals, as plate-warmers) and which were furnished with
hooks at different heights to support the roasting- [74] spits. Hanging from the mantle-shelf was a short curtain to hold the smoke in
check; and on the shelf were various utilitarian ornaments: a row of

six covered jars, of old faience, ranging in holding capacity from a gill to three pints, each lettered with the name of its contents—saffron, pepper, tea, salt, sugar, flour; and with these some burnished copper vessels, and a coffee-pot, and a half-dozen of the tall brass or pewter lamps for burning olive-oil—which long ago superseded the primitive *calèu*, dating from Roman or from still earlier times, and which now themselves practically have been superseded by lamps burning petroleum.

To the right of the fire-place was the stone sink, with shelves above it on which was a brilliant array of polished copper and tin pots and pans. To the left was the covered bread-trough, above which hung the large salt and flour boxes and the grated bread-closet—this last looking like a child's crib gone wrong—all of dark wood ornamented with carving and with locks and hinges of polished iron. On the opposite side of the room, matching these pieces in colour and [75] carving and polished iron-work, were a tall buffet and a tall clock—the clock of so insistent a temperament that it struck in duplicate, at an interval of a minute, the number of each hour. A small table stood in a corner, and in ordinary times the big dining-table was ranged along one of the walls, with benches on each side of it supplemented by rush-bottomed chairs. Near the bread-trough was hung a long-armed steel-balance with a brass dish suspended by brass chains, all brilliant from scouring with soap and sand; an ancient fowling-piece rested in wooden crutches driven between the stones on one side of the clock, and on the other side was hung a glittering copper warming-pan—a necessary comfort here of cold nights in fireless rooms. By way of ornament, three or four violently-colored lithographs were tacked against the walls, together with a severely formal array—a pyramidal trophy—of family photographs.

Excepting the warming-pan and the two arm-chairs ordinarily in the chimney-corners, there was no provision in the room for bodily ease or comfort: a lack unperceived [76] by its occupants, but which an American house-wife—missing her many small luxuries and conveniences—would have found sharply marked.

XI

The crèche, around which the children were gathered in a swarm, was built up in one corner; and our coming was the signal for the first of the ceremonies, the lighting of the crèche candles, to begin. In this all the children had a part—making rather a scramble of it, for there was rivalry as to which of them should light the most—and in a moment a constellation of little flames covered the Bethlehem hill-side and brought into bright prominence the Holy Family and its strange attendant host of quite impossible people and beasts and birds.

The laying of the yule-log followed; a ceremony so grave that it has all the dignity of, and really is, a religious rite. The buzz of talk died away into silence as Elizo's father, the oldest man, took by the hand and led out [77] into the court-yard where the log was lying his great-grandson, the little Tounin, the youngest child: it being the rule that the nominal bearers of the *cacho-fiò* to the hearth shall be the oldest and the youngest of the family—the one personifying the year that is dying, the other the year new-born. Sometimes, and this is the prettiest rendering of the custom, the two are an old, old man and a baby carried in its mother's arms—while between them the real bearers of the burden walk.

In our case the log actually was carried by Marius and Esperit; but the tottering old man clasped its forward end with his thin feeble hands, and its hinder end was clasped by the plump feeble hands of the tottering child. Thus, the four together, they brought it in through the doorway and carried it thrice around the room, circling the supper-table and the lighted candles; and then, reverently, it was laid before the fire-place—that still sometimes is called in Provençal the *lar*.

ELIZO'S OLD FATHER

There was a pause, while the old man filled out a cup of *vin cue*; and a solemn hush fell upon the company, and all heads were bowed, [78] as he poured three libations upon the log, saying with the last: "In the name of the Father, and of the Son, and of the Holy Ghost!" — and then cried with all the vigor that he could infuse into his thin and quavering old voice:

> Cacho-fiò,
> Bouto-fiò!
> Alègre! Alègre!
> Diéu nous alègre!
> Calèndo vèn! Tout bèn vèn!
> Diéu nous fague la gràci de vèire l'an que vèn,
> E se noun sian pas mai, que noun fuguen pas mens!

> Yule-log,
> Catch fire!
> Joy! Joy!
> God gives us joy!
> Christmas comes! All good comes!

> May God give us grace to see the coming year,
> And if we are not more, may we not be less!

As he ended his invocation he crossed himself, as did all the rest; and a great glad shout was raised of "Alègre! Alègre!" as Marius and Esperit—first casting some fagots of vine-branches on the bed of glowing coals—placed the yule-log upon the fire. Instantly [79] the vines blazed up, flooding the room with brightness; and as the yule-log glowed and reddened everybody cried

> Cacho-fiò,
> Bouto-fiò!
> Alègre! Alègre!

again and again—as though the whole of them together of a sudden had gone merry-mad!

In the midst of this triumphant rejoicing the bowl from which the libation had been poured was filled afresh with *vin cue* and was passed from hand to hand and lip to lip—beginning with the little Tounin, and so upward in order of seniority until it came last of all to the old man—and from it each drank to the new fire of the new year.

Anciently, this ceremony of the yule-log lighting was universal in Provence, and it is almost universal still; sometimes with a less elaborate ritual than I have described, but yet substantially the same: always with the libation, always with an invocation, always with the rejoicing toast to the new fire. But [80] in modern times—within the last century or so—another custom in part has supplanted it in Marseille and Aix and in some few other towns. This is the lighting of candles at midnight in front of the crèche; a ceremony, it will be observed, in which new fire still bears the most important part.

One of my Aix friends, the poet Joachim Gasquet, has described to me the Christmas Eve customs which were observed in his own home: the Gasquet bakery, in the Rue de la Cepède, that has been handed down from father to son through so many hundreds of years that even its owners cannot tell certainly whether it was in the fourteenth or the fifteenth century that their family legend of good baking had its rise. As Monsieur Auguste, the *contre-maître* of the bakery, opened the great stone door of the oven that I might peer into its hot depths, an historical cross-reference came into my mind that made me realize its high antiquity. Allowing for difference of longitude, the *contre-maître* who was Monsieur Auguste's remote predecessor was lifting the morning's baking out of that oven at the very moment when Columbus [81] saw through the darkness westward the lights of a new world!

In the Gasquet family it was the custom to eat the Great Supper in the oven room: because that was the heart, the sanctuary, of the house; the place consecrated by the toil which gave the family its livelihood. On the supper-table there was always a wax figure of the Infant Christ, and this was carried just before midnight to the living-room, off from the shop, in one corner of which the crèche was set up. It was the little Joachim whose right it was, because he was the youngest, the purest, to carry the figure. A formal procession was made. He walked at its head, a little chap with long curling golden hair, between his two grandfathers; the rest followed in the order of their age and rank: his two grandmothers, his father and mother, Monsieur Auguste (a dashing blade of a young baker then) with the maid-servant, and the apprentices last of all. A single candle was carried by one of his grandfathers into the dark room — the illumination of which, that night, could come only from the new fire kindled before the crèche. Precisely at [82] midnight — at the moment when all the clocks of Aix striking together let loose the Christmas chimes — the child laid the holy figure in the manger, and then the candles instantly were set ablaze.

Sometimes there would be a thrilling pause of half a minute or more while they waited for the bells: the child, with the image in his hands, standing before the crèche in the little circle of light; the others grouped behind him, and for the most part lost in dark shadow cast by the single candle held low down; those nearest to the crèche holding matches ready to strike so that all the candles might be lighted at once when the moment came. And then all the bells together would send their voices out over the city heavenward; and his mother would say softly, "Now, my little son!"; and the room would flash into brightness suddenly—as though a glory radiated from the Christ-Child lying there in the manger between the ox and the ass.

Every evening throughout the Christmas season the candles were relighted before this Christmas shrine, and there the members of the family said in common their evening [83] prayer; and when the time came for taking down the crèche those parts of it which were not preserved for the ensuing year—the refuse scraps of wood and pasteboard and moss and laurel—were burned (this is the orthodox general custom) with something of the flavour of a rite; not cast into the household fire nor the bakery oven, but saved from falling into base places by being consumed in a pure fire of its own.

XII

While our own more orthodox yule-log ceremonial was in progress, the good Elizo and Janetoun—upon whom the responsibility of the supper rested—evidently were a prey to anxious thoughts. They whispered together and cast uneasy glances toward the chimney, into the broad corners of which the various cooking vessels had been moved to make way for the *cacho-fiò*; and the moment that the cup of benediction had passed their lips they precipitated themselves upon the fire-place and replaced the [84] pots and pans for a final heating upon the coals.

The long table had been set before our arrival and was in perfect readiness—covered with a fine white linen cloth, sacredly reserved for use at high festivals, that fairly sparkled in the blaze of light cast by the overhanging petroleum lamp. Yet the two ceremonial candles, one at each end of the table, also were lighted; and were watched anxiously as the supper went on: for should the wick of one of the Christmas candles fall before the supper is ended, the person toward whom it points in falling will pass from earth before the Christmas feast is set again. But Misè Fougueiroun, to guard against this ominous catastrophe, had played a trick on Fate by providing wax candles with wicks so fine that they wasted away imperceptibly in their own flame.

Beside those fateless candles were the harvest harbingers, the plates on which was growing Saint Barbara's grain—so vigorous and so freshly green that old Jan rubbed his hands together comfortably as he said to the Vidame: "Ah, we need have no fears for the [85] harvest that is coming in this blessed year!" In the centre of the table, its browned crust slashed with a cross, was the great loaf of Christmas bread, *pan Calendau;* on which was a bunch of holly tied with the white pith of rushes—the "marrow" of the rush, that is held to be an emblem of strength. Old Jan, the master of the house, cut the loaf into as many portions as there were persons present; with one double-portion over to be given to some poor one in charity—"the portion of the good God." It is of a miraculous nature, this blessed bread: the sailors of Provence carry morsels of it with them on their voyages, and by strewing its crumbs upon the troubled waters stay the tempests of the sea.

For the rest, the table had down its middle a line of dishes—many of them old faience of Moustiers, the mere sight of which would have thrilled a collector's heart—heaped with the nougat and the other sweets over the making of which our housekeeper and her lieutenants so soulfully had toiled. And on the table in the corner were fruits and nuts and wines.

Grace always is said before the Great Sup [86] per—a simple formula ending with the prayer of the yule-log that if another year there are no more, there may be no less. It is the custom that this blessing shall be asked by the youngest child of the family who can speak the words: a pretty usage which sometimes makes the blessing go very queerly indeed. Our little Tounin came to the front again in this matter, exhibiting an air of grave responsibility which showed that he had been well drilled; and it was with quite a saintly look on his little face that he folded his hands together and said very earnestly: "God bless all that we are going to eat, and if we are no less next year may we be no more!" At which everybody looked at Janetoun and laughed.

In our seating a due order of precedence was observed. Old Jan, the head of the family, presided, with the Vidame and myself on his right and with Elizo's father and mother on his left; and thence the company went downward by age and station to the foot of the table, where were grouped the servants from the Château and the workmen on the farm. But no other distinction was made. [87] All were served alike and all drank together as equals when the toasts were called. The servers were Elizo and Janetoun, with Nanoun and Magali for assistants; and those four, although they took their places at the table when each course had been brought on, had rather a Passover time of it: for they ate as it were with their loins girded and with full or empty dishes imminent to their hands.

The stout Nanoun—whose robust body thrills easily to superstitious fears—was still farther handicapped in her own eating by her zealous effort so to stuff the family cat as to give that animal no excuse for uttering evil-portending miaus. For it is well known that should the family cat fall to miauing on Christmas Eve, and especially while the supper is in progress, very dreadful things surely will happen to the family during the ensuing year. Fortunately Nanoun's preventive measures averted this calamity; yet were they like to have overshot their mark. Only the cat's natural abstemiousness saved her that night from dying of a surfeit—and in agony surely provocative of the very cries which Nanoun sought to restrain! [88]

As I have said, the Great Supper must be "lean," and is restricted to certain dishes which in no wise can be changed; but a rich leanness is possible in a country where olive-oil takes the place of animal fat in cooking, and where the accumulated skill of ages presides over the kitchen fire. The principal dish is the *raïto*—a ragout made of delicately fried fish served in a sauce flavoured with wine and capers—whereof the tradition goes back a round twenty-five hundred years: to the time when the Phokæan housewives brought with them to Massalia (the Marseille of to-day) the happy mystery of its making from their Grecian homes. But this excellent dish was not lost to Greece because it was gained to Gaul: bearing the same name and made in the same fashion it is eaten by the Greeks of the present day. It usually is made of dried codfish in Provence, where the cod is held in high esteem; but is most delicately toothsome when made of eels.

The second course of the Great Supper also is fish, which may be of any sort and served in any way—in our case it was a perch-like

[89] variety of dainty pan-fish, fresh from the Rhône. A third course of fish sometimes is served, but the third course usually is snails cooked in a rich brown sauce strongly flavoured with garlic. The Provençal snails, which feed in a *gourmet* fashion upon vine-leaves, are peculiarly delicious—and there was a murmur of delight from our company as the four women brought to the table four big dishes full of them; and for a while there was only the sound of eager munching, mixed with the clatter on china of the empty shells. To extract them, we had the strong thorns, three or four inches long, of the wild acacia; and on these the little brown morsels were carried to the avid mouths and eaten with a bit of bread sopped in the sauce—and then the shell was subjected to a vigorous sucking, that not a drop of the sauce lingering within it should be lost.

To the snails succeeded another dish essentially Provençal, *carde.* The carde is a giant thistle that grows to a height of five or six feet, and is so luxuriantly magnificent both in leaf and in flower that it deserves a place among ornamental plants. The edible [90] portion is the stem—blanched like celery, which it much resembles, by being earthed-up—cooked with a white sauce flavoured with garlic. The garlic, however, is a mistake, since it overpowers the delicate taste of the carde—but garlic is the overlord of all things eatable in Provence. I was glad when we passed on to the celery, with which the first section of the supper came to an end.

The second section was such an explosion of sweets as might fly into space should a comet collide with a confectioner's shop— nougat, *fougasso*, a great *poumpo*, compotes, candied-fruits, and a whole nightmare herd of rich cakes on which persons not blessed with the most powerful organs of digestion surely would go galloping to the country of dreadful dreams. This was prodigality; but even the bare requirements of the case were lavish, the traditional law of the Great Supper ordaining that not fewer than seven different sweets shall be served. Misè Fougueiroun, however, was not the person to stand upon the parsimonious letter of any eating law. Here had been her opportunity, and she had run amuck through all the range of sugary things! [91]

Of the dessert of nuts and fruit the notable features were grapes and winter-melons. Possibly because they are an obscure survival of some Bacchic custom connected with the celebration of the winter solstice, the grapes are considered a very necessary part of the Great Supper; but as Provençal grapes are of a soft substance and soon wither, though a world of care is taken to preserve a few bunches until Christmas, this part of the feast usually is a ceremony rather than a satisfaction.

But our melons were a pure vegetable delight. These winter-melons are a species of cantaloupe, but of a firmer texture than the summer fruit, sowed late in the season and laid away a little green on beds of straw in cool and dark and well-aired rooms. Thus cared for, they will keep until the end of January; but they are preserved especially for Christmas, and few survive beyond that day. They are of American origin: as I discovered quite by chance while reading a collection of delightful letters, but lately published, written near three hundred years ago by Dr. Antoine Novel; that Provençal naturalist, [92] whom Buffon quotes under the wrongly Latinized name of Natalis, sometime physician to the Duke of Medina-Sidonia in Spain. He was a rolling stone of a naturalist, the excellent Novel; but his gatherings were many, and most of them were for the benefit of his beloved Provence. It was from "Sainct Luquar," under date of March 24, 1625, that he wrote to his friend Peiresc in Aix: "I send you by the Patron Armand a little box in which are two specimens of ore ... and ten sorts of seeds of the most exquisite fruits and flowers of the Indies; and to fill the chinks I have put in the seeds of winter-melons." And in a letter of June 12th, following, he wrote: "I hope that you have received my letter sent by the Patron Armand of Martigues, who sailed in Holy Week for that town, by whom I sent you some seeds of exquisite fruits and flowers of the Indies, together with two specimens of ore, the one from Potosí and the other from Terra-Firma, and also a box of seven winter-melons of that country." And so the winter-melons came into Provence from somewhere on the Spanish Main. I could wish that my gentleman had been a [93] bit more definite in his geography. As he leaves the matter, his melons may have come from anywhere between the Orinoco and Florida; and down in that region somewhere, no doubt, they still are to be found.

With the serious part of the supper we drank the ordinary small wine diluted with water; but with the dessert was paraded a gallant company of dusty bottles containing ancient vintages which through many ripening years had been growing richer by feeding upon their own excellence in the wine-room of the Mazet or the cellar of the Château. All were wines of the country, it being a point of honour in Provençal households of all degrees that only from Provençal vineyards—or from the near-by vineyards of Languedoc—shall come the Christmas wines. Therefore we drank rich and strong Tavel, and delicate Ledenon, and heavy Frontignan—the cloyingly-sweet Mouscat de Maroussa—and home-made champagne (the *clairette*, with a superabundance of pop and fizz but undeniably cider-like), and at last, for a climax, old Châteauneuf-du-Pape: the dean of the Provençal vinous faculty, rich, smooth, delicate, [94] with a slightly aromatic after-taste that the dallying bees bring to the vine-blossoms from the blossoms of the wild-thyme. Anciently it filled the cups over which chirped the sprightly Popes of Avignon; and in later times, only forty years back, it was the drink of the young Félibrien poets—Mistral, Roumanille, Aubanel, Mathieu and the rest—while they tuned and set a-going their lyres. But it is passing into a tradition now. The old vines, the primitive stock, were slain by the phylloxera, and the new vines planted to replace them do not produce a wine like that over which Popes and poets once were gay. Only in rich old cellars, such as that of Vièlmur, may still be found a bin or two of dust-grey Papal veterans: survivors of the brave army that has gurgled its life out in a happy past!

XIII

But the material element of the Great Supper is its least part. What entitles it to the augmenting adjective is its soul: that subtle essence of peace and amity for which [95] the word Christmas is a synonym in all Christian lands. It is the rule of these family gatherings at Christmas time in Provence that all heartburnings and rancours, which may have sprung up during the year, then shall be cut down; and even if sometimes they quickly grow again, as no doubt they do now and then, it makes for happiness that they shall be thus banished from the peace-feast of the year.

Janetoun and one of her sisters-in-law were the only members of our party who had a hatchet to bury; and the burial was over so quickly—being but an extra hug and an explosion of kisses—that I should have known nothing about it but for the over-long tongue of Misè Fougueiroun: who, in a kindly way, is as thorough-going a gossip as ever lived. Of all things in the world to quarrel about, this quarrel had grown out of a spirited difference of opinion as to how the heel of a knitted stocking should be turned! But the matter had come to be quite of a seriousness, and all the family breathed freer when those resounding peace-kisses were given and received. Actually, as I happened to learn [96] later, the reconciliation was pushed to such an extreme that each of them incontinently adopted the other's knitting creed—with the curious result that they now are in a fair way to have a fresh quarrel for next Christmas out of the same matter on inverted lines! It was before the lighting of the yule-log that the feud of the stocking heels thus happily (even though only temporarily) was pacified, and the family festival was cloudless from first to last.

When the serious part of the supper had been disposed of and the mere palate-tickling period of the dessert had come, I was much interested in observing that the talk—mainly carried on by the elders—was turned with an obviously deliberate purpose upon family history; and especially upon the doings of those who in the past had brought honour upon the family name. And I was still more interested when, later, the Vidame informed me that it is the Provençal custom at the Christmas festival for the old thus to instruct the young and so to keep family tradition alive. No doubt there is in this a dim survival of ancestor-worship; but I should be glad to see [97] so excellent a relic of paganism preserved in the Christmas ritual of my own land.

The chief ancestral glory of the family of the Mazet is its close blood-relationship with the gallant André Étienne: that drummer of the Fifty-first Demi-brigade of the Army of Italy who is commemorated on the frieze of the Panthéon, and who is known and honoured as the "Tambour d'Arcole" all over France. It was delightful to listen to old Jan's telling of the brave story: how this André, their own kinsman, swam the stream under the enemy's fire at Arcolo with his drum on his back and then drummed his fellow-soldiers on to victory; how the First Consul awarded him the drum-sticks of honour, and later—when the Legion of Honour was founded—gave him the cross; how they carved him in stone, drumming the charge, up there on the front of the Panthéon in Paris itself; how Mistral, the great poet of Provence, had made a poem about him that had been printed in a book; and how, crowning glory, they had set up his marble statue in Cadenet—the little town, not far from Avignon, where he was born! [98]

Old Jan was not content with merely telling this story—like a true Provençal he acted it: swinging a supposititious drum upon his back, jumping into an imaginary river and swimming it with his head in the air, swinging his drum back into place again, and then—*Zóu!*—starting off at the head of the Fifty-first Demi-brigade with such a rousing play of drum-sticks that I protest we fairly heard the rattle of them, along with the spatter of Italian musketry in the face of which André Étienne beat that gallant *pas-de-charge*!

It set me all a-thrilling; and still more did it thrill those other listeners who were of the Arcolo hero's very blood and bone. They clapped their hands and they shouted. They laughed with delight. And the fighting spirit of Gaul was so stirred within them that at a word—the relations between France and Italy being a little strained just then—I verily believe they would have been for marching in a body across the south-eastern frontier!

Elizo's old father was rather out of the running in this matter. It was not by any relative of his that the drum-sticks of honour had been won; and his thoughts, after wander [99] ing a little, evidently settled down upon the strictly personal fact that his thin old legs were cold. Rising slowly from the table, he carried his plate to the fire-place; and when he had arranged some live coals in one of the baskets of the waist-high andirons he rested the plate above them on the iron rim: and so stood there, eating contentedly, while the warmth from the glowing yule-log entered gratefully into his lean old body and stirred to a brisker pulsing the blood in his meagre veins. But his interest in what was going forward revived again—his legs being, also, by that time well warmed—when his own praises were sounded by his daughter: in the story of how he stopped the runaway horse on the very brink of the precipice at Les Baux; and how his wife all the while sat calmly beside him in the cart, cool and silent, and showing no sign of fear.

When Elizo had finished this story she whispered a word to Magali and Nanoun that sent them laughing out of the room; and presently Magali came back again arrayed in the identical dress which had been worn by the heroine of the adventure—who [100] had perked and plumed herself not a little while her daughter told about it—when the runaway horse so nearly had galloped her off the Baux rock into Eternity. It was the Provençal costume—with full sleeves and flaring cap—of sixty years back; but a little gayer than the strict Arles dress of that period, because her mother was not of Arles but of Beaucaire. It was not so graceful, especially in the head-dress, as the costume of the present day; nor nearly so becoming—as Magali showed by looking a dozen years older after putting it on. But Magali, even with a dozen years added, could not but be charming; and I think that the little old bowed grandmother—who still was a bit of a coquette at eighty—would have been better pleased had she been spared this encounter with what must have seemed to her very like a meeting with her own young ghost, raised suddenly from the depths of the distant past.

MAGALI

By long experience, gained on many such occasions, the Vidame knew that the culminating point of the supper would be reached when the family drummer swam the river and headed the French charge at Arcolo. [101] Therefore had he reserved until a later period, when the excitement incident to the revival of that honourable bit of family history should have subsided, a joy-giving bomb-shell of his own that he had all ready to explode. An American or an Englishman never could have fired it without something in the way of speech-making; but the Vidame was of a shy temper, and speech-making was not in his line. When the chatter caused by Magali's costuming had lulled a little, and there came a momentary pause in the talk, he merely reached diagonally across the table and touched glasses with Esperit and said simply: "To your good health, Monsieur the Superintendent of the Lower Farm!"

It was done so quietly that for some seconds no one realized that the Vidame's toast brought happiness to all the household, and to two of its members a life-long joy. Esperit, even, had his glass almost to his lips before he understood to what he was drinking; and then his understanding came through the finer nature of Magali—who gave a quick deep sob as she buried her face in the buxom Nanoun's bosom and encircled that aston [102] ished young person's neck with her arms. Esperit went pale at that; but the hand did not tremble in which he held his still-raised glass, nor did his voice quaver as he said with a deep earnestness: "To the good health of Monsieur le Vidame, with the thanks of two very happy hearts!"—and so drained his wine.

A great danger puts no more strain upon the nerves of a man of good fibre than does a great joy; and it seemed to me that Esperit's absolute steadiness, under this sudden fire of happiness, showed him to be made of as fine and as manly stuff as went to the making of his kinsman who beat the *pas-de-charge* up the slope at Arcolo at the head of the Fifty-first Demi-brigade.

But nothing less than the turbulence of the whole battle of Arcolo—not to say of that whole triumphant campaign in Italy—will suffice for a comparison with the tumult that arose about our supper-table when the meaning of the Vidame's toast fairly was grasped by the company at large! I do not think that I could express in words—nor by any less elaborate method of illustration than a kinetoscope—the state of excitement into [103] which a Provençal will fly over a matter of absolutely no importance at all; how he will burst forth into a very whirlwind of words and gestures about some trifle that an ordinary human being would dispose of without the quiver of an eye. And as our matter was one so truly moving that a very Dutchman through all his phlegm would have been stirred by it, such a tornado was set a-going as would have put a mere hurricane of the tropics to open shame!

Naturally, the disturbance was central over Esperit and Magali and the Vidame. The latter—his kind old face shining like the sun of an Easter morning—gave back with a good will on Magali's cheeks her kisses of gratitude; and exchanged embraces and kisses with the elder women; and went through such an ordeal of violent hand-shaking that I trembled for the integrity of his arms. But as for the young people, whom everybody embraced over and over again with a terrible energy, that they came through it all with whole ribs is as near to being a miracle as anything that has happened in modern times! [104]

Gradually the storm subsided—though not without some fierce after-gusts—and at last worked itself off harmlessly in song: as we returned to the ritual of the evening and took to the singing of noëls—the Christmas canticles which are sung between the ending of the Great Supper and the beginning of the midnight mass.

XIV

The Provençal noëls—being some real, or some imagined, incident of the Nativity told in verse set to a gay or tender air—are the crèche translated into song. The simplest of them are direct renderings of the Bible narrative. Our own Christmas hymn, "While shepherds watched their flocks by night," is precisely of this order; and, indeed, is of the very period when flourished the greatest of the Provençal noël writers: for the Poet Laureate Nahum Tate, whose laurel this hymn keeps green, was born in the year 1652 and had begun his mildly poetic career while Saboly still was alive. [105]

But most of the noëls—*nouvè*, they are called in Provençal—are purely imaginative: quaintly innocent stories created by the poets, or taken from those apocryphal scriptures in which the simple-minded faithful of Patristic times built up a warmly coloured legend of the Virgin's life and of the birth and childhood of her Son. Sometimes, even, the writers stray away entirely from a religious base and produce mere roistering catches or topical songs. Such are those Marseille noëls which are nothing more than Pantagruelian lists of succulent dishes proper to Christmas time—frankly ending, in one case, with the materialistic query: "What do I care for the future, now that my belly is well lined?" It was against such "bacchanals of noël" that the worthy Father Cotton preached in Marseille in the year 1602: but the flesh and the devil always have had things pretty much their own way in that gay city, and he preached in vain. And at Aix-en-Provence the most popular noël of all that were sung in the cathedral was a satirical review of the events of the year: that as time went on grew to be more and more of a scandal, until at [106] last the Bishop had to put a stop to it in the year 1653.

The Provençaux have been writing noëls for more than four hundred years. One of the oldest belongs to the first half of the fifteenth century and is ascribed to Raimond Féraud; the latest are of our own day—by Roumanille, Crousillat, Mistral, Girard, Gras, and a score more. But only a few have been written to live. The memory of many once-famous noël-writers is preserved now either mainly or wholly by a single song. Thus the Chanoine Puech, who died at Aix almost two hundred and fifty years ago, lives in the noël of the Christ-Child and the three gypsy fortune-tellers—which he stole, I am sorry to say, from Lope de Vega. The Abbé Doumergue, of Aramon, who flourished at about the same period, is alive because of his "March of the Kings": that has come ringing down through the ages set to Lulli's magnificent "March of Turenne"; and it is interesting to note that Lulli is said to have found his noble motive in a Provençal air. Antoine Peyrol, who lived only a little more than a century ago, and who "in our good city of Avignon [107] was a carpenter and wood-seller and a simple-hearted singer of Bethlehem" (as Roumanille puts it) has fared better, more than a dozen of his noëls surviving to be sung each year when "the nougat bells" (as they call the Christmas chimes in Avignon) are ringing in his native town. And, on the other hand, as though to strike a balance between fame and forgottenness, there are some widely popular noëls—as "C'est le bon lever"—of which the authorship absolutely is unknown; while there are still others—as the charming "Wild Nightingale"—which belong to no one author, but have been built up by unknown farm-house poets who have added fresh verses and so have passed on the amended song.

The one assured immortal among these musical mortalities is Nicolas Saboly: who was born in Monteux, close by Avignon, in the year 1614; who for the greater part of his life was chapel-master and organist of the Avignon church of St. Pierre; who died in the year 1675; and who lies buried in the choir of the church which for so long he filled with his own heaven-sweet harmonies. [108] Of his beautiful life-work, Roumanille has written: "As organist of the church of St. Pierre, Saboly soon won a great and beautiful renown as a musician; but his fame and his glory have come to him because of the blessed thought that he had of composing his marvellous noëls. Yet it was not until the year 1658, when he himself was fifty-four years old, that he decided to tie together and to publish his first sheaf of them. From that time onward, every year until his end, a fresh sheaf of from six to a dozen appeared; and, although no name went with them, all of his townsfolk knew that it was their own Troubadour of the Nativity who made them so excellent a gift just as the nougat bells began to ring. The organ of St. Pierre, touched by his master hand, taught the gay airs to which the new noëls were cast. And all Avignon presently would be singing them, and soon the chorus would swell throughout the Comtat and Provence. The inimitable Troubadour of Bethlehem died just as he had tied together the eighth of his little sheaves.... His noëls have been reprinted many times; and, thanks be to [109] God, they will be printed again and again forever!" [3]

In addition to being a genius, Saboly had the good fortune to live in one of the periods of fusing and recasting which give to genius its opportunity. He was born at the very time when Claude Monteverde was taking those audacious liberties with harmony which cleared the way for the transition from the old tonality to the new; and he died before the great modern masters had set up those standards which composers of our time must either accept or defy. He certainly was influenced by the then new Italian school; indeed, from the fourteenth century, when music began to be cultivated in Avignon, the relations between that city and Italy were so close that the first echoes of Italian musical innovators naturally would be heard there. Everywhere his work shows, as theirs does, a searching for new methods in the domain [110] of modulation, and a defiance of the laws of transformation reverenced by the formal composers of his time. Yet he did his searching always on his own lines and in his own way.

Nor was his original genius lessened by his willingness at times to lay hands on the desirable property of other people—since his unlawful acquisitions received always a subtle touch which really made them his own. He knew well how to take the popular airs of the moment—the gavotte or minuet or vaudeville which every one was singing: the good old airs, as we call them now, which then were the newest of the new—and how to infuse into them his own personality and so to fit them like a glove to his own noëls. Thus, his Twelfth noël is set to an air composed by Lulli for the drinking song, "Qu'ils sont doux, bouteille jolie," in Molière's "Médecin mal-gré lui"; and those who are familiar with the music of his time will be both scandalized and set a-laughing by finding the uses to which he has put airs which began life in far from seemly company. But his forays were made from choice, not from necessity, and the best of his noëls are his own. [111]

Saboly's music has a "go" and a melodic quality suggestive of the work of Sir Arthur Sullivan; but it has a more tender, a fresher, a purer note, even more sparkle, than ever Sullivan has achieved. In his gay airs the attack is instant, brilliant, overpowering—like a glad outburst of sweet bells, like the joyous laughter of a child—and everything goes with a dash and a swing. But while he thus loved to harmonize a laugh, he also could strike a note of infinite tenderness. In his pathetic noëls he drops into thrillingly plaintive minors which fairly drag one's heart out—echoes or survivals, possibly (for this poignant melody is not uncommon in old Provençal music), of the passionately longing love-songs with which Saracen knights once went a-serenading beneath castle windows here in Provence.

Nor is his verse, of its curious kind, less excellent than his music. By turns, as the humour takes him, his noëls are sermons, or deli-cate religious fancies, or sharp-pointed satires, or whimsical studies of country-side life. One whole series of seven is a history of the Nativity (surely the quaintest and the [112] gayest and the tenderest oratorio that ever was written!) in which, in music and in words, he is at his very best. Above all, his noëls are local. His background always is his own country; his characters—Micolau the big shep-herd, gossip Guihaumeto, Tòni, Christòu, and the rest—always are Provençaux: wearing Provençaux pink-bordered jackets, and white hats bedizened with ribbons, and marching to Bethlehem to the sound of the *galoubet* and *tambourin*. It is from Avignon, out by the Porte Saint Lazare, that the start for Bethlehem is made by his pil-grim company; the Provençal music plays to cheer them; they stamp their feet and swing their arms about, because the mistral is blowing and they are desperately cold. It is a simplicity half laughable, half pathetic—such as is found in those Mediæval pictures which represent the Apostles or the Holy Family in the garb of the artist's own time and country, and above the walls of Bethlehem the church spire of his own town.

This naïve local twist is not peculiar to Saboly. With very few exceptions all Provençal noëls are packed full of the same delightful [113] anachronisms. It is to Provençal shepherds that the Herald Angel appears; it is Provençaux who compose the *bregado*, the pilgrim company, that starts for Bethlehem; and Bethlehem is a village, always within easy walking distance, here in Provence. Yet it is not wholly simplicity that has brought about this shifting of the scene of the Nativity from the hill country of Judæa to the hill country of Southeastern France. The life and the look of the two lands have much in common; and most impressively will their common character be felt by one who walks here by night beneath the stars.

Here, as in the Holy Land, winding ways pass out from olive-orchards, and on across dry reaches of upland broken by outcropping rocks and scattered trees and bushes and sparsely thatched with short dry grass. Through the silence will come now and then the tinkle of sheep-bells. Sometimes a flock will be seen, dimly in the starlight, feeding beside the road; and watching, from an overlooking standpoint on a rock or little upswelling hill-top, will be its shepherd: a tall muffled figure showing black against the [114] loom of the sky. And it all is touched, in the star-haze of those sombre solitudes, with the poetic realism of unreality; while its deeper meaning is aroused by the stone crosses, telling of Calvary, which are found at every parting of the ways. Told to simple dwellers in such a land the Bible story was neither vague nor remote. They knew its setting because their own surroundings were the same. They practised the shepherd customs; the ass was their own beast of burden; the tending of vines and fig-trees and olive-orchards was a part of their daily lives. And so, naturally, the older noël writers without any thought of anachronism, and the modern writers by poetic instinct made complete their translation of the story of the Nativity into their vernacular by transferring its scene to their own land.

XV

It was with Saboly's "Hòu, de l'houstau!" that our singing began. It is one of the series in his history of the Nativity and is the most popular of all his noëls: a [115] dialogue between Saint Joseph and the Bethlehem inn-keeper, that opens with a sweet and plaintive long-drawn note of supplication as Saint Joseph timorously calls:

> "O-o-oh, there, the house! Master! Mistress!
> Varlet! Maid! Is *no* one there?"

And then it continues with humble entreaties for shelter for himself and his wife, who is very near her time; to which the host replies with rough refusals for a while, but in the end grants grudgingly a corner of his stable in which the wayfarers may lie for the night.

Esperit and Magali sang this responsively; Magali taking Saint Joseph's part—in which, in all the noëls, is a strain of feminine sweetness and gentleness. Then Marius and Esperit, in the same fashion, sang the famous "C'est le bon lever": a dialogue between an Angel and a Shepherd, in which the Angel—as becomes so exalted a personage—speaks French, while the Shepherd speaks Provençal.

"It's high time to get up, sweet shepherd," the Angel begins; and goes on to tell that "in Bethlehem, quite near this place," the Saviour of the world has been born of a Virgin. [116]

"Perhaps you take me for a common peasant," the Shepherd answers, "talking to me like that! I am poor, but I'd have you to know that I come of good stock. In old times my great-great-grandfather was mayor of our village! And who are you, anyway, fine sir? Are you a Jew or a Dutchman? Your jargon makes me laugh. A virgin mother! A child god! No, never were such things heard!"

But when the Angel reiterates his strange statement the Shepherd's interest is aroused. He declares that he will go at once and steal this miraculous child; and he quite takes the Angel into his confidence—as though standing close to his elbow and speaking as friend to friend. In the end, of course, he is convinced of the miracle,

and says that he "will get the ass and set forth" to join the worship-
pers about the manger at Bethlehem.

There are many of these noëls in dialogue; and most of them are
touched with this same quality of easy familiarity with sacred subjects, and abound in turns of broad humour which render them not
a little startling from our nicer point of view. But they never are
[117] coarse, and their simplicity saves them from being irreverent;
nor is there, I am sure, the least thought of irreverence on the part of
those by whom they are sung. I noticed, though, that these lively
numbers were the ones which most hit the fancy of the men; while
the women as plainly showed their liking for those of a finer spirit
in which the dominant qualities were pathos and grace.

Of this latter class is Roumanille's rarely beautiful noël "The Blind
Girl" ("La Chato Avuglo") — that Magali sang with a tenderness
which set the women to crying openly, and which made the older
men cough a little and look suspiciously red about the eyes. Of all
the modern noëls it has come closest to and has taken the strongest
hold upon the popular heart: this pathetic story of the child "blind
from her birth" who pleads with her mother that she also may go
with the rest to Bethlehem, urging that though she cannot see "the
lovely golden face" she still may touch the Christ-Child's hand.

> And when, all thrilling, to the stable she was come
> She placed the little hand of Jesus on her heart —
> And saw him whom she touched!
> [118]

"THE BLIND GIRL"—NOËL

But without the music, and with only these crude translations in which is lost also the music of the words, I feel that I am giving very much less than the true effect of these Provençal Christmas songs. To be appreciated, to be understood, they must be heard as I heard them: sung by that Christmas company, with Magali's tenderly vibrant voice leading the chorus in which every one of those singing Provençaux joined. Even the old grandfather—still standing at the fire-place—marked the time of the music with the knife that he held in his hand; and his thin old voice piped in with the others, and had a gay or a tender ring in it with the changing melody, for all that it was so cracked and shrill.

I am persuaded, so thoroughly did they all enjoy their own carolling, that the singing of noëls would have gone on until broad daylight had it not been for the intervention of the midnight mass. But the mass of Christmas Eve — or, rather, of Christmas morning — is a matter not only of pleasure but of obligation. Even those upon whom churchly requirements at other times rest [119] lightly rarely fail to attend it; and to the faithful it is the most touchingly beautiful — as Easter is the most joyous — church festival of the year.

By eleven o'clock, therefore, we were under way for our walk of a mile or so down the long slope of the hill side to the village: a little clump of houses threaded by narrow crooked streets and still in part surrounded by the crusty remnant of a battlemented wall — that had its uses in the days when robber barons took their airings and when pillaging Saracens came sailing up the slack-water lower reaches of the Rhône. Down the white road in the moonlight we went in a straggling company, while more and more loudly came to us through the crisp night air the sound of the Christmas bells.

Presently some one started a very sweet and plaintive noël: fairly heart-wringing in its tender beseeching and soft lament, yet with a consoling under-note to which it constantly returned. I think, but I am not sure, that it was Roumanille's noël telling of the widowed mother who carried the cradle of her own baby to the Virgin, that the Christ- [120] Child might not lie on straw. One by one the other voices took up the strain, until in a full chorus the sorrowingly compassionate melody went thrilling through the moonlit silence of the night.

And so, singing, we walked by the white way onward; hearing as we neared the town the songs of other companies coming up, as ours was, from outlying farms. And when they and we had passed in through the gateways — where the townsfolk of old lashed out against their robber Infidel and robber Christian enemies — all the black little narrow streets were filled with an undertone of murmuring voices and an overtone of clear sweet song.

XVI

On the little Grande Place the crowd was packed densely. There the several streams of humanity pouring into the town met and mingled; and thence in a strong current flowed onward into the church. Coming from the blackness without—for the tall houses surrounding the Grande Place cut off [121] the moonlight and made it a little pocket of darkness—it was with a shock of splendour that we encountered the brightness within. All the side-altars were blazing with candles; and as the service went on, and the high-altar also flamed up, the whole building was filled with a soft radiance—save that strange luminous shadows lingered in the lofty vaulting of the nave.

After the high-altar, the most brilliant spot was the altar of Saint Joseph, in the west transept; beside which was a magnificent crèche—the figures half life-size, beautifully modelled, and richly clothed. But there was nothing whimsical about this crèche: the group might have been, and very possibly had been, composed after a well-painted "Nativity" by some artist of the late Renaissance.

The mass was the customary office; but at the Offertory it was interrupted by a ceremony that gave it suddenly an entirely Mediæval cast: of which I felt more fully the beauty, and the strangeness in our time, because the Vidame sedulously had guarded against my having knowledge of it in advance. This [122] was nothing less than a living rendering of the Adoration of the Shepherds: done with a simplicity to make one fancy the figures in Ghirlandojo's picture were alive again and stirred by the very spirit that animated them when they were set on canvas four hundred years ago.

By some means only a little short of a miracle, a way was opened through the dense crowd along the centre of the nave from the door to the altar, and up this way with their offerings real shepherds came—the quaintest procession that anywhere I have ever seen. In the lead were four musicians—playing upon the *tambourin*, the *galoubet*, the very small cymbals called *palets*, and the bagpipe-like *carlamuso*—and then, two by two, came ten shepherds: wearing the long brown full cloaks, weather-stained and patched and mended, which seem always to have come down through many generations and which never by any chance are new; carrying tucked beneath their arms their battered felt hats browned, like their cloaks, by long warfare with sun and rain; holding in one hand a lighted candle and in the other a staff. The [123] two leaders dispensing with staves and candles, bore garlanded baskets; one filled with fruit—melons, pears, apples, and grapes—and in the other a pair of doves: which with sharp quick motions turned their heads from side to side as they gazed wonderingly on their strange surroundings with their bright beautiful eyes.

Following came the main offering: a spotless lamb. Most originally, and in a way poetically, was this offering made. Drawn by a mild-faced ewe, whose fleece had been washed to a wonder of whiteness and who was decked out with bright-coloured ribbons in a way to unhinge with vanity her sheepish mind, was a little two-wheeled cart—all garlanded with laurel and holly, and bedizened with knots of ribbon and pink paper roses and glittering little objects such as are hung on Christmas-trees in other lands. Lying in the cart placidly, not bound and not in the least frightened, was the dazzlingly-white lamb, decked like the ewe with knots of ribbon and wearing about its neck a red collar brilliant to behold. Now and then the ewe would turn to look at it, and in response to [124] one of those wistful maternal glances the little creature stood up shakily on its unduly long legs and gave an anxious baa! But when a shepherd bent over and stroked it gently, it was reassured; lying down contentedly again in its queer little car of triumph, and thereafter through the ceremony remaining still. Behind the car came ten more shepherds; and in their wake a long double line of country-folk, each with a lighted candle in hand. There is difficulty, indeed, in keeping that part of the demonstration within bounds, because it is esteemed an honour and a privilege to walk in the procession of the offered lamb.

Slowly that strange company moved toward the altar, where the ministering priest awaited its coming; and at the altar steps the bearers of the fruit and the doves separated, so that the little cart might come between them and their offering be made complete, while the other shepherds formed a semi-circle in the rear. The music was stilled, and the priest accepted and set upon the altar the baskets; and then extended the paten that the shepherds, kneeling, might kiss it in token of their [125] offering of the lamb. This completed the ceremony. The *tambourin* and *galoubet* and *palets* and *car-lamuso* all together struck up again; and the shepherds and the lamb's car passed down the nave between the files of candle-bearers and so out through the door.

Within the past sixty years or so this naïve ceremony has fallen more and more into disuse. But it still occasionally is revived—as at Barbentane in 1868, and Rognonas in 1894, and repeatedly within the past decade in the sheep-raising parish of Maussane—by a curé who is at one with his flock in a love for the customs of ancient times. Its origin assuredly goes back far into antiquity; so very far, indeed, that the airs played by the musicians in the procession seem by comparison quite of our own time: yet tradition ascribes the composition of those airs to the good King René, whose happy rule over Provence ended more than four centuries ago.

Another custom of a somewhat similar character, observed formerly in many of the Provençal churches, was the grouping before the altar at the mass on Christmas Day [126] of a young girl, a choir-boy, and a dove: in allegorical representation of the Virgin Mary, the Angel Gabriel, and the Holy Ghost. But the assembly of this quaint little company long since ceased to be a part of the Christmas rite.

XVII

When the stir caused by the coming and the going of the shepherds had subsided, the mass went on; with no change from the usual observance, until the Sacrament was administered, save that there was a vigorous singing of noëls. It was congregational singing of a very enthusiastic sort—indeed, nothing short of gagging every one of them could have kept those song-loving Provençaux still—but it was led by the choir, and choristers took the solo parts. The most notable number was the famous noël in which the crowing of a cock alternates with the note of a nightingale; each verse beginning with a prodigious cock-a-doodle-d-o-o! and then rattling along to the gayest of gay airs. The nightingale was not a brilliant success; but [127] the cock-crowing was so realistic that at its first outburst I thought that a genuine barn-yard gallant was up in the organ-loft. I learned later that this was a musical *tour-de-force* for which the organist was famed. A buzz of delight filled the church after each cock-crowing volley; and I fancy that I was alone in finding anything odd in so jaunty a performance within church walls. The viewpoint in regard to such matters is of race and education. The Provençaux, who are born laughing, are not necessarily irreverent because even in sacred places they sometimes are frankly gay.

Assuredly, there was no lack of seemly decorum when the moment came for the administration of the Sacrament; which rite on Christmas Eve is reserved to the women, the men communing on Christmas Day. The women who were to partake—nearly all who were present—wore the Provençal costume, but of dark colour. Most of them were in black, save for the white chapelle, or kerchief, and the scrap of white which shows above the ribbon confining the knotted hair. But before going up to the altar each placed upon [128] her head a white gauze veil, so long and so ample that her whole person was enveloped in its soft folds; and the women were so many, and their action was with such sudden unanimity, that in a moment a delicate mist seemed to have fallen and spread its silvery whiteness over all the throng.

Singly and by twos and threes those palely gleaming figures moved toward the altar, until more than a hundred of them were crowded together before the sanctuary rail. Nearest to the rail, being privileged to partake before the rest, stood a row of black-robed Sisters—teachers in the parish school—whose sombre habits made a vigorous line of black against the dazzle of the altar, everywhere aflame with candles, and by contrast gave to all that sweep of lustrous misty whiteness a splendour still softer and more strange. And within the rail the rich vestments of the ministering priests, and the rich cloths of the altar, all in a flood of light, added a warm colour-note of gorgeous tones.

Slowly the rite went on. Twenty at a time the women, kneeling, ranged themselves at the rail; rising to give room to others when [129] they had partaken, and so returning to their seats. For a full half hour those pale lambent figures were moving ghost-like about the church, while the white-veiled throng before the altar gradually diminished until at last it disappeared: fading from sight a little at a time, softly—as dream-visions of things beautiful melt away.

Presently came the benediction: and all together we streamed out from the brightness of the church into the wintry darkness—being by that time well into Christmas morning, and the moon gone down. But when we had left behind us the black streets of the little town, and were come out into the open country, the star-haze sufficed to light us as we went onward by the windings of the spectral white road: for the stars shine very gloriously in Provence.

We elders kept together staidly, as became the gravity of our years; but the young people—save two of them—frolicked on ahead and took again with a will to singing noëls; and from afar we heard through the night-stillness, sweetly, other home-going com [130] panies singing these glad Christmas songs. Lingering behind us, following slowly, came Esperit and Magali—to whom that Christmas-tide had brought a life-time's happiness. They did not join in the joy-songs, nor did I hear them talking. The fullest love is still.

And peace and good-will were with us as we went along the white way homeward beneath the Christmas morning stars.

Saint-Remy-de-Provence,
September, 1896.

[133]

A Feast-Day on the Rhône

I

This water feast-day was a part of the biennial pilgrimage to the Sainte-Estelle of the Félibrige and the Cigaliers: the two Félibrien societies maintained in Paris by the children of the South of France. Through twenty-three dreary months those expatriated ones exist in the chill North; in the blessed twenty-fourth month—always in burning August, when the melons are luscious ripe and the grapes are ripening, when the sun they love so well is blazing his best and the whole land is a-quiver with a thrilling stimulating heat—they go joyously southward upon an excursion which has for its climax the great Félibrien festival: and then, in their own gloriously hot Midi, they really live!

By a semi-right and by a large courtesy, we of America were of this gay party. Four years earlier, as the official representatives [134]

78

of an American troubadour, we had come upon an embassy to the troubadours of Provence; and such warm relations had sprung up between ourselves and the poets to whom we were accredited that they had ended by making us members of their own elect body: the Society of the Félibrige—wherein are united the troubadours of these modern times. As Félibres, therefore, it was not merely our right but our duty to attend the festival of the Sainte-Estelle; and our official notification in regard to this meeting—received in New York on a chill day in the early spring-time—announced also that we were privileged to journey on the special steamboat chartered by our brethren of Paris for the run from Lyons to Avignon down the Rhône.

II

We were called at five o'clock in the morning. Even the little birds of Lyons were drowsy at that untoward and melancholy hour. As I slowly roused myself I heard their sleepy twitterings out in the trees [135] on the Cours du Midi—and my sympathies were with them. There are natures which are quickened and strengthened by the early day. Mine is not such. I know of nothing which so numbs what I am pleased to term my faculties as to be *particeps criminis* in the rising of the sun.

But life was several shades less cheerless by the time that we left the Hôtel Univers—which I ever shall remember gratefully because it ministered so well, even in the very midst of the driving bustle of the Lyons Exposition, to our somewhat exacting needs—and went down to the river side. Already the mists of morning had risen, and in their place was the radiant sunshine of the Midi: that penetrating, tingling sunshine which sets the blood to dancing and thence gets into the brain and breeds extravagant fancies there which straight-way are uttered as substantial truths—as M. Daudet so often has told us; and also, when writing about this his own dearly-loved birth-land, so often has demonstrated in his own text.

Yet had we come to the boat while still in the lowering mood be-gotten of our intem [136] perate palterings with the dawn we must have yielded quickly to the infectious cheerfulness which obtained on board the *Gladiateur*. Even a Grey Penitent would have been moved, coming unawares into that gay company, to throw off his *cagoule* and to dance a saraband. From end to end the big *Gladiateur* was bright with bunting — flags set in clusters on the great paddle-boxes, on the bow, on the stern — and the company thronging on board was living up to the brightness of the sunshine and the flags.

For they were going home, home to their dear South, those poet exiles: and their joy was so strong within them that it almost touched the edge of tears. I could understand their feeling because of a talk that I had had three days before, in Paris, with Baptiste Bonnet: up in his little apartment under the mansard, with an outlook over the flowers in the window-garden across roof-tops to Notre Dame. Bonnet could not come upon this expedition — and what love and longing there was in his voice while he talked to us about the radiant land which to him was forbidden but which we so soon were to [137] see! To know that we were going, while he remained behind, made us feel like a brace of Jacobs; and when Madame Bonnet made delicious tea for us — "because the English like tea," as she explained with a clear kindliness that in no wise was lessened by her misty ethnology — we felt that so to prey upon their hospitality in the very moment that we were making off with their birthright was of the blackest of crimes. But because of what our dear Bonnet had said, and of the way in which he had said it, I understood the deep feeling that underlay the exuberant gayety of our boat-mates — and it seemed to me that there was a very tender note of pathos in their joy.

They were of all sorts and conditions, our boat-mates: a few famous throughout the world, as the player Mounet-Sully, the painter Benjamin Constant, the prose poet Paul Arène; many famous throughout France; and even in the rank and file few who had not raised themselves above the multitude in one or another of the domains of art. And all of them were bound together in a democratic [138] brotherhood, which yet — because the absolute essential to membership in it was genius — was an artistic aristocracy. With their spiritual honours had come to many of them honours temporal; indeed, so plentiful were the purple ribbons of the Palms and the red rosette of the Legion — with here and there even a Legion button — as to suggest that the entire company had been caught out without umbrellas while a brisk shower of decorations passed their way. A less general, and a far more picturesque, decoration was the enamelled cigale worn by the Cigaliers: at once the emblem of their Society, of the Félibrien movement, and of the glowing South where that gayest of insects is born and sings his life out in the summer days.

Most of the poets came to the boat breakfastless, and their first move on board was toward the little cabin on deck wherein coffee was served. The headwaiter at the improvised breakfast table—as I inferred not less from his look and manner than from his ostentatiously professed ignorance of his native tongue—was an English duke in reduced circumstances; and his assistants, I [139] fancy, were retired French senators. Indeed, those dignified functionaries had about them an air of high comedy so irresistible, and so many of the ladies whom they served were personages of the Odéon or the Comédie Française, that only the smell of the coffee saved the scene from lapsing into the unrealism of the realistic stage.

Seven o'clock came, but the *Gladiateur* remained passive. At the gang-plank were assembled the responsible heads of the expedition—who were anything but passive. They all were talking at once, and all were engaged in making gestures expressive of an important member of the party who had been especially charged to be on hand in ample time; who had outraged every moral principle by failing to keep his appointment; whose whereabouts could not be even remotely surmised; whose absence was the equivalent of ruin and despair—a far less complex series of concepts, I may add, than a southern Frenchman is capable of expressing with his head and his body and his hands.

It was the pianist.

A grave Majoral, reaching down to the [140] kernel of the matter, solved the difficulty with the question: "Have we the piano?"

"We have."

"Enough!" cried the Majoral. "Let us go."

In a moment the gang-plank was drawn aboard; the lines were cast off; the great paddle-wheels began to turn; the swift current laid hold upon us—and the *Gladiateur*, slipping away from the bank, headed for the channel-arch of the Pont-du-Midi. The bridge was thronged with our friends of Lyons come down to say goodbye to us. Above the parapet their heads cut sharp against the morning glitter of the sun-bright sky. All together they cheered us as we, also cheering, shot beneath them: and then the bridge, half hidden in the cloud of smoke from our huge funnel, was behind us—and our voyage was begun.

III

Of all the rivers which, being navigable, do serious work in the world the Rhône is the most devil-may-care and light-hearted. [141] In its five hundred mile dash down hill from the Lake of Geneva to the Mediterrænean its only purpose—other than that of doing all the mischief possible—seems to be frolic fun. And yet for more than two thousand years this apparently frivolous, and frequently ma-levolent, river has been very usefully employed in the service of mankind.

In the misty barbaric ages before history fairly began, and in the early times of the Roman domination, the Rhône was the sole high-way into northern Gaul from the Mediterrænean; later, when the Gallic system of Roman roads had been constructed, it held its own fairly well against the two roads which paralleled it—that on the east bank throughout almost its entire length, and that on the west bank from Lyons southward to a point about opposite to the pre-sent Montélimar; in the semi-barbarous Middle Ages—when the excitements of travel were increased by the presence of a robber-count at every ford and in every mountain-pass—it became again more important than the parallel highways on land; and in our own day the conditions of Roman times, relatively speaking, [142] are restored once more by steamboats on the river and railways on the lines of the ancient roads. And so, having served these several mas-ters, the Rhône valley of the present day is stored everywhere with remnants of the barbarism, of the civilization, and of the semi-barbarism which successively have been ploughed under its surface before what we have the temerity to call our own civilization began. Keltic flints and pottery underlie Roman ruins; just beneath the soil, or still surviving above it, are remains of Roman magnificence; and on almost all the hill-tops still stand the broken strongholds of the robber nobles who maintained their nobility upon what they were lucky enough to be able to steal. Naturally—those ruined castles, and the still-existent towns of the same period, being so conspicuously in evidence—the flavour of the river is most distinctly Mediæval; but a journey in this region, with eyes open to perceive as well as to see, is a veritable descent into the depths of the ancient past.

Indeed, the *Gladiateur* had but little more than swung clear from Lyons—around the long curve where the Saône and the Rhône [143] are united and the stream suddenly is doubled in size—than we were carried back to the very dawn of historic times. Before us, stretching away to the eastward, was the broad plain of Saint-Fons—once covered with an oak forest to which Druid priests bearing golden sickles came from the Île Barbe at Yule-tide to gather mistletoe for the great Pagan feast; later, a battle-field where Clodius Albinus and Septimius Severus came to a definite understanding in regard to the rulership of Gaul; later still, the site of a pleasure castle of the Archbishops of Lyons, and of the Villa Longchêne to which light-hearted Lyons' nobles came. Palace and Villa still are there—the one a Dominican school, the other a hospital endowed by the Empress Eugénie: but the oaks and the Druids and the battle are only faint legends now.

I am forced to admit that never a thought was given to that aggregation of antiquities by the too-frivolous passengers aboard the *Gladiateur*. At the very moment when we were steaming through those Gallo-Roman and Mediæval latitudes there was a burst of [144] music from the piano that fired our light-headed company as a spark fires a mine. The music was the air of "La Coupe," the Félibrien Anthem, and instantly a hundred voices took up the song. When this rite was ended, the music shifted to a livelier key and straightway a farandole was formed. On the whole, a long and narrow steamboat is not an especially good place for a farandole; but the leader of that one—a young person from the Odéon, whose hair came down repeatedly but whose exceptionally high spirits never came down at all—was not one of the sort whom difficulties deter. At the head of the long line of dancers—a living chain held together by clasped hands—she caracoled and curveted up and down the narrow passes of the boat; and after her, also caracoling and curveting, came the chain: that each moment grew in length as volunteers joined it, or (in keeping with farandole customs) as the less vivacious members of the party were seized upon and forcibly impressed into its ranks. And so we farandoled clear away to Givors.

It took the place of a master of ceremonies, [145] our farandole, and acted as an excellent solvent of formalities. Yet even without it there would have been none of the stiffness and reserve which would have chilled a company assembled under like conditions in English-speaking lands. Friendliness and courtesy are characteristics of the French in general; and especially did our American contingent profit by those amiable traits that day on the Rhône. Save for a slight correspondence with a single member of the party, all aboard the boat were strangers to us; but in that kindly atmosphere, before we had time to fancy that we were outsiders, we found ourselves among friends.

Givors slipped by almost unnoticed in the thick of the farandole: a little town hung out to sun in long strips upon terraces rising from the water-side; the walls and tiled roofs making a general effect of warm greys and yellows dashed with the bright greens of shrubs and trees and gardens and the yellow green of vines. 'Tis a town of some commercial pretensions: the gateway of a canal a dozen miles long leading up through the valley of the little river Gier to iron-works and [146] coke-works and glass-works tucked away in the hills. The canal was projected almost a century and a half ago as a connecting channel between the Rhône and the Loire, and so between the Atlantic and the Mediterrænean; wherefore the Canal of the Two Oceans was, and I suppose continues to be, its high-sounding name. But the Revolution came, and the digging never extended beyond that first dozen miles; and thus it is that the Canal of the Two Oceans, as such, is a delusion, and that the golden future which once lay ahead of Givors now lies a long way astern. Yet the town has an easy and contented look: as though it had saved enough from the wreck of its magnificent destiny to leave it still comfortably well to do.

Before we fairly had passed it, and while the farandole was dying out slowly, there crashed down upon us a thunderous outburst of song: as though an exceptionally large-lunged seraph were afloat immediately above us in the open regions of the air. Yet the song was of a gayer sort than seraphs, presumably, are wont to sing; and its method, distinctly, was that of the modern operatic [147] stage. In point of fact, the singer was not a seraph, but an eminent professor in a great institution of learning and a literary authority of the first rank—whose critical summary of French literature is a standard, and whose studies of Beaumarchais and Le Sage have been crowned by the Academy. In sheer joyousness of spirit that eminent personage had betaken himself to the top of the port paddle-box, and thence was suffering his mountain-cleaving voice to go at large: so quickening was the company in which he found himself; so stimulating was the racy fervour of his own Southern sun!

IV

From Givors the river runs almost in a straight line to Vienne. On both shores rise round-crested wooded hills—the foothills of the parallel ranges of mountains by which the wide valley is shut in. Down this perspective, commandingly upon a height, is seen the city—misty and uncertain at first, but growing clearer and clearer, as the boat [148] nears it, until the stone-work of man and the rock-work of nature become distinct and the picture is complete in all its parts: the time-browned mass of houses on the hill-top; the tower of Philip the Fair; over all, the huge façade of Saint Maurice—an ogival wonder that for centuries was the cathedral church of the Primates of Gaul.

After Marseille, Vienne makes as handsome pretensions to age as are made by any town in France. The tradition of its founding lies hidden in the mists of heroic legend, and is the more momentous because it is so impressively vague. Over its very name the etymologists wrangle with such violence that one is lost in amazement at their ill-tempered erudition; and over its structure the archæologists—though a bit more civil to each other—are almost as violently at cross-purposes. The best esteemed of those antiquary gentry—at least the one whom I esteem the most, because I like the fine boldness of his claim—is the Dominican chronicler Lavinius: who says flatly that Vienne was founded thirteen centuries before the dawn of the Christian era by a contemporary of Moses, one King [149] Allobrox—a Keltic sovereign descended from Hercules in a right line! That is a good beginning; and it has the merit of embodying the one fact upon which all of the testy antiquaries are agreed:

that Vienne the Strong, as folk called it in those days, was a flourishing town long before Lyons was built or Paris even thought of, and an age or two before the Romans came over into Gaul.

When at last they did come, the Romans transformed the town into a great city—the metropolis of the region lying between Geneva and Marseille; and so adorned it with noble buildings—temples, forum, circus, theatre, aqueducts, baths—and so enriched it with all manner of works of art, that it came to be known as Vienne the Beautiful throughout the civilized world. One temple, approximately perfect, has survived to us from that time; and one statue—the famous Crouching Venus: and it seems fair enough to accept Vienne's beauty as proved by these. Moreover, painting and music were cultivated there, together with the other arts: and from all that the historians have to tell us it would [150] appear that the Roman citizens of that city lived softly and well.

In the dark ages of Mediæval Christianity most of the beauties of Vienne vanished: being destroyed outright, or made over into buildings pertaining to the new faith and the new times. A pathetic little attempt, to be sure, was made by the Viennese to hold fast to their comfortable Paganism—when Valentinian II. was slain, and the old rites were restored, at the end of the fourth century; but it was a mere flash in the pan. The tendencies of the times were too strong to be resisted, and presently the new creed rode down the old. Then it was that Vienne was called Vienne the Holy—because, while losing nothing of her splendours temporal, she gained great store of splendours spiritual: whereof the culmination was that famous Council, at the beginning of the fourteenth century, which crushed the Templars and gave over their possessions to the Crown. While the Council deliberated, Philip the Fair "watched his case," as the lawyers would put it, from the village of Sainte-Colombe—across the river—where he was quartered with his court [151] in the convent of the Cordeliers; and in Sainte-Colombe, the next year, he built the tower that was to safeguard the royal domains against the aggressions of the Archbishops: whose too-notorious holiness was making them overbold.

And nowadays Vienne is a mean little town; a withered kernel in the shell of its former grandeur; a mere sousprefecture; scarcely more than a manufacturing suburb of Lyons. In the tower of Philip the Fair are a cheap restaurant, and a factory of macaroni, and a carpenter-shop. It is enough to make the spirits of the Roman emperors indignant and the bones of the Archbishops rattle dismally in their graves. No longer either strong, or beautiful, or holy, they call it Vienne the Patriotic, now. A city must be something, of course—and patriotism is an attribute that may be had for the claiming, in these days.

But the saving grace of poetry, at least of the love of poetry, still abides in Vienne: as was proved in a manner mightily tickling to our self-complacency as we swept past the town. Taking the place of the stone bridge [152] that was built in Roman times—and so well built that it was kept in service almost down to our own day— a suspension bridge here spans the stream: and the poets and the poet-lovers of Vienne were all a-swarm upon it, their heads and shoulders rising in an animated crenellation above its rail, in waiting for our galley to go by. While we still were a hundred yards away up stream there was a bustling movement among them; and then a bouquet, swinging at the end of a light line, was lowered away swiftly—the bright flowers flashing in the sunlight as they swayed and twirled. Our brethren had calculated to a nicety where our boat would pass. Right over the bow came the bouquet, and fairly into the eager hands stretched out for it—while a great cheer went up from the grateful poets in the boat that was echoed by the generous poets in the air. And the prettiest touch of all was the garland of verses that came to us with the flowers: to bid us welcome and to wish us God-speed on our way. Truly, 'twas a delicately fine bit of poetic courtesy. No troubadour in the days of Vienne the Holy (the holiness was not of an [153] austere variety) could have cast a more graceful tribute upon the passing galley of the debonaire Queen Jeanne.

V

Before Vienne the river cuts its way narrowly through the rock, and on each side the banks lift high above the stream. Far above us was the town, rising in terraces to where was the citadel in the days of Vienne the Strong. We had a flying glimpse of it all as we flashed past, sped by the current and our great wheels; and then the valley widened again, and soft meadows bordered by poplars and gay with yellow flowers lay between us and the mountain ranges rising to right and left against the sky. Here and there along the banks, where an outcrop of rock gave good holding-ground, were anchored floating grist-mills carrying huge water-wheels driven by the current—the wooden walls so browned with age that they seemed to have held over from the times when the archbishops, lording it in Vienne, took tithes of millers' toll. [154]

We were come into a country of corn and wine. The mills certified to the corn; and as we swung around the curves of the river or shot down its reaches we met long lean steamboats fighting against the current under heavy ladings of big-bellied wine-casks—on their genial way northward to moisten thirsty Paris throats. Off on the right bank was the ancient manor of Mont-Lys, where begins the growth of the Côtes-Rôties: the famous red and white wines, called the *brune* and the *blonde*, which have been dear to bottle-lovers for nearly two thousand years: from the time when the best of them (such as now go northward to Paris) went southward to the Greek merchants of Marseille and so onward to Rome to be sold for, literally, their weight in gold. And as to the melons and apricots which grow hereabouts, 'tis enough to say that Lyons bereft of them would pine and die.

The softly-swelling banks, capped by the long lines of yellow-green poplars, slipped by us at a gallop; while the mountains in the background, seen through the haze of flickering leaves, seemed to stand still. It was the [155] most peaceful of landscapes: but there was endless fighting thereabouts in former times. In an Early Christian way the archbishops of Vienne ravaged among the Protestants; between whiles the robber-counts, without respect to creed, ravaged among the travelling public with a large-minded impartiality; and, down in the lowest rank of ravagers, the road-agents of the period stole all that their betters left for them to steal. As we passed the little town of Condrieu—where a lonely enthusiast stood up on the bank and waved a flag at us—we saw overtopping it, on a fierce little craggy height, the ruined stronghold of its ancient lords. Already, in the thirty miles or thereabouts that we had come since leaving Lyons, we had passed a half-dozen or more warlike remnants of a like sort; and throughout the run to Avignon they continued at about the rate of one in every five miles.

Singly, the histories of these castles are exceedingly interesting studies in Mediæval barbarism; but collectively they become a wearisomely monotonous accumulation of horrors. Yet it is unfair to blame the lords [156] of the castles for their lack of originality in crime. With the few possible combinations at their command, the Law of Permutation literally compelled them to do the same things over and over again: maintaining or sustaining sieges ending in death with or without quarter for the besieged; leading forays for the sake of plunder, with or without the incentive of revenge; crushing peasant rebellions by hanging such few peasants as escaped the sword; and at all times robbing every unlucky merchant who chanced to come their way. It was a curious twist, that reversion to savagery, from the Roman epoch: when the Rhône Valley was inhabited by a civilized people who encouraged commerce and who had a genuine love for the arts. And, after all—unless they had some sort of pooling arrangement—the robber lords in the mid-region of the Rhône could not have found their business very profitable. Merchants travelling south from Lyons must have been poor booty by the time that they had passed Vienne; and merchants travelling north from Avignon, similarly, must have been well fleeced by the time that they were come to the [157] Pont-Saint-Esprit. Indeed, the lords in the middle of the run doubtless were hard put to it at times to make any sort of a living at all. Nor could the little local stealing that went on have helped them much—since, their respective castles being not more than five miles asunder, each of them in ordinary times was pulled up short in his ravaging at the end of two miles and a half. In brief, the business was overcrowded in all its branches, and badly managed beside. The more that I look into the history of that time the more am I convinced that mediævalism, either as an institution or as an investment, was not a success.

Condrieu is a dead little town now. As a seat of thieving industry its importance disappeared centuries ago; and its importance as a boating town—whence were recruited a large proportion of the Rhône boatmen—vanished in the dawn of the age of steam. They were good fellows, those Condrieu boatmen, renowned for their bravery and their honesty throughout the river's length. Because of their leather-seated breeches they were nicknamed "Leather-tails"; but their more sailor- [158] like distinction was their tattooing: on the fore-arm a flaming heart pierced with an arrow, symbol of their fidelity and love; on the breast a cross and anchor, symbols of their faith and craft. From Roman times downward until railways came, the heavy freighting of central France has been done by boat upon the Rhône—in precisely the same fashion that flat-boat freighting was carried on upon the Mississippi and its tributaries—and three or four of the river towns were peopled mainly by members of the boating guilds. Trinquetaille, the western suburb of Arles, still shows signs of the nautical tastes of its inhabitants in the queer sail-or-like exterior and interior adornments of its houses: most noticea-ble of which is the setting up on a house-top of a good-sized boat full-rigged with mast and sails.

The survivors of the boating period nowadays are few. Five years ago I used to see whenever I crossed to Trinquetaille a little group of old boatmen sitting at the end of the bridge on a long bench that was their especial property. They moved stiffly and slowly; their white heads were bowed breastward; [159] their voices were cracked with age. Yet they seemed to be cheery together, as they basked in the hot sunshine—that warmed only comfortably their lean old bodies—and talked of ancient victories over sand-bars and rapids: and the while looked southward over the broad Rhône wa-ter toward the sea. No doubt they held in scorn their few succes-sors—one where of old were a hundred—who navigate the Rhône of to-day, clipped of its perils by dykes and beacons, in boats driven by steam.

Yet these modern mariners, charged with the care of the great steamboats two and three hundred feet long, are more heroic char-acters than were the greatest of the old-time navigators. The finest sight that I saw in all that day aboard the *Gladiateur* was our pilot at his post as he swung us around certain of the more dangerous of the curves: where rocks or sand-bars narrowed the channel closely and where a fall in the river-bed more than usually abrupt made the current fiercely strong. In such perilous passes he had behind him in a row at the long tiller—these boats are not steered by a wheel forward, [160] but by a tiller at the stern—two, three, and at one turn four men. He himself, at the extreme end of the tiller, stood firmly posed and a little leaning forward, his body rigid, his face set in resolute lines, his eyes fixedly bent upon the course ahead; behind him the others, elately poised in readiness to swing their whole weight with his on the instant that his tense energy in repose flashed into energy in action as the critical turn was made — the whole group, raised above us on the high quarter-deck, in relief against the deep blue sky. Amy, or another of the Southern sculptors, will be moved some day, I hope, to seize upon that thrilling group and to fasten it forever in enduring bronze.

VI

As we approached the bridge of Serrières it was evident that another demonstration in our honour was imminent. On the bridge a small but energetic crowd was assembled, and we could see a bouquet pendent from a cord descending toward the point [161] where our boat was expected to pass. The projectors of that floral tribute cheered us finely as we came dashing toward them; and up in our bows was great excitement — which suddenly was intensified into anguish as we perceived that our admirers had made a miscalculation: a fateful fact that was anticipated and realized almost in the same instant — as we saw the bouquet level with our deck but forty feet away a-beam! Yet good luck saved the day to us. As we shot the bridge we also rounded a curve, and a moment after the bow of the long *Gladiateur* had gone wide of the bouquet the stern had swung around beneath it and it was brought safe aboard. In the same breath we had passed under and beyond the bridge and were sending up stream to our benefactors our cheers of thanks.

When the discovery was made that a bottle was enshrined among the flowers, and that upon the bottle was an inscription — necessarily a sonnet, as we impulsively decided — our feeling toward Serrières was of the warmest. Without question, those generous creatures had sent us of their best, and with a [162] posy of verse straight from their honest hearts. Only poets ministering to poets could have conceived so pretty a scheme. But the eager group that surrounded the Majoral who held the bottle flew asunder in wrath as he read out loudly, in place of the expected sonnet, these words: "Quinine prepared by Cuminat at Serrières"! And then our feeling toward Serrières grew much less warm. Yet I am not sure that Cuminat was moved only by the sordid wish to advertise at our expense his preparation of quinine. I am disposed to credit him in part with a helpful desire to check the fever rising in the blood of our boat-load of Southerners who each moment—as they slid down that hill-side of a river—were taking deeper and stronger drafts of the heady sunshine of their own Southern sun. On the other hand, I am forced to admit that had his motive been pure benevolence his offering would not have been so pitiably scant.

But the people of Tournon—to which generous town, and to the breakfast provided by its cordial inhabitants, we came an hour before noon—entreated us with so prodigal a liberality in the matter of bottles that the [163] questionable conduct of the Serrières apothecary quickly faded from our minds. In ancient times Tournon had a black reputation for its evil-dealing with chance wayfarers along the Rhône, and one's blood runs cold with mere thought of the horrors which went on there in the times of the religious wars. But very likely because of an honest desire to live down its own bad record—which I mention here rather to its present credit than to its past shame—it now seems determined to balance matters by manifesting toward passing travellers the most obliging courtesy in the world. Certainly, we poets—coming thither famished, and going thence full fed and sleekly satisfied—had cause that day to bless its name.

As we came galloping around a curve in the river—I cannot insist too strongly upon the dashing impetuosity that was the constant buoyant undertone of our voyage—this Tournon the blessed shot up before us perked out upon a bold little hill thrust forward into the stream: a crowd of heavily-built houses rising around a church or two and a personable campanile, with here and [164] there bits of crenellated ramparts, and higher still the tough remnant of a castle still fit to do service in the wars. Indeed, it all was so good in colour—with its blendings of green and grey shot with warm yellow tones; and its composition was so excellent—with its sweep upward from the river to the castle battlements—that to my American fancy (used rather to Mediæval semblances than to Mediæval realities) it seemed to be temporarily escaped from an exceptionally well-set operatic stage.

THE LAND-
ING-PLACE AT TOURNON

All Tournon was down at the water-side to meet us, and on the
landing-stage was the very Mayor: a lean and tri-coloured man who
took off his hat comprehensively to our whole company in a magnificent bow. Notables were with him—the Sous-Prefect, the Mayor
of Tain, the Adjoint, leading citizens—who also bowed to us; but
not with a bow like his! Laurel garlands decorated the landing-
stage; more laurel garlands and the national colours made gay the
roadway leading up the bank; and over the roadway was a laurel-

wreathed and tri-coloured triumphal arch—all as suitable to welcoming poets and patriots, such [165] as we were, as suitable could be. As the *Gladiateur* drew in to the bank there was a noble banging of *boîtes*—which ancient substitute for cannon in joy-firing still are esteemed warmly in rural France—and before the Mayor spoke ever a word to us the band bounded gallantly into the thick of the "Marseillaise."

With the *boîte* banging fitfully, with the band in advance playing "La Coupe," the tri-coloured Mayor led off with the most distinguished lady of our company upon his arm: and away we all went, under the triumphal arch and up the garlanded roadway two by two—as though Tournon were a Rhône-side Ararat and we were the animals coming out of the Ark. Our entry was a veritable triumph; and we endeavoured (I think successfully) to live up to it: walking stately through the narrow streets, made narrower by the close-packed crowds pressing to see so rare a poetic spectacle; through the cool long corridors of the Lycée; and so out upon a prettily dignified little park—where, at a triad of tables set within a garlanded enclosure beneath century-old plane-trees, our [166] breakfast was served to us to the accompaniment of bangs from the *boîte* and musical remarks from the band. And all Tournon, the while, stood above us on a terrace and sympathetically looked on.

In its adaptation to the needs of travelling poets the breakfast was a master-stroke. It was simple, substantial, delicious; and in its accompanying prodigal outpouring of red and white Hermitage, Cornas, and Saint-Péray, the contrast with the bottle-niggardliness of Serrières was bravely marked. The Hermitage, from the hill-sides directly across the river from Tournon, around the town of Tain, scarcely lives up to its heroic tradition just now—the phylloxera having destroyed the old vines, planted by the hermit of blessed memory, and the new vines having in them still the intemperate strength of youth. Yet is it a sound rich wine, in a fair way to catch up again with its ancient fame.

While we feasted, the *boîte* and the band took turns in exploding with violence; and when, with the filet, the band struck up "La Coupe" away we all went with it in a chorus that did not die out entirely until well along [167] in the galantine. The toasts came in

with the ices, and on the basis of the regional champagne, Saint-
Péray — sweet, but of good flavour — that cracked its corks out with
the irregular volleyings of a line of skirmishers firing in a fog. The
tri-coloured Mayor on behalf of Tournon, and Paul Arène and delightful Sextius Michel on behalf of the Félibrige and the Cigaliers,
and M. Maurice Faure, the Deputy, on behalf of the Nation at large,
exchanged handsome compliments in the most pleasing way; and
the toasts which they gave, and the toasts which other people gave,
were emphasized by a rhythmic clapping of hands in unison by the
entire company — in accordance with the custom that obtains always
at the feasts of the Félibres.

But that was no time nor place for extended speech-making. All
in a whiff our feast ended; and in another whiff we were up and
off — whisking through the Lycée corridors and the crowded streets
and under the triumphal arch and so back on board the *Gladiateur*.
The Mayor, always heroically ablaze with his patriotic scarf of office, stood on the landing-stage — like a courteous Noah in [168]
morning dress seeing the animals safely up the Ark gang-plank —
and made to each couple of us one of his stately bows; the *boîte* fired
a final salvo of one round; the band saluted us with a final outburst
of the "Marseillaise"; everybody, ashore and afloat, cheered — and
then the big wheels started, the current caught us and wrenched us
apart from all that friendliness, and away we dashed down stream.

VII

Long before we came abreast of it by the windings of the river we
saw high up against the sky-line, a clear three hundred feet above
the water, all that is left of the stronghold of Crussol — still called by
the Rhône boatmen "the Horns of Crussol," although the two towers
no longer shoot out horn-like from the mountain-top with a walled
war-town clinging about their flanks. One Géraud Bartet, a cadet of
the great house of Crussol — of which the representative nowadays
is the Duc d'Uzès — built this eagle's nest in the year 1110; but it did
not become a place [169] of importance until more than four hundred years later, in the time of the religious wars.

On the issue of faiths the Crussols divided. The head of the house
was for the Pope and the King; the two cadets were for God and the
Reform. Then it was that the castle (according to an over-sanguine

chronicler of the period) was "transformed into an unconquerable stronghold"; and thereafter—always for the advancement of Christianity of one sort or another—a liberal amount of killing went on beneath its walls. In the end, disregarding the fact that it was unconquerable, the castle was captured by the Baron des Adrets—who happened at the moment to be on the Protestant side—and in the interest of sound doctrine all of its defenders were put to the sword. Tradition declares that "the streams of blood filled one of the cisterns, in which this terrible Huguenot had his own children bathed 'in order,' as he said, 'to give them strength and force and, above all, hatred of Catholicism.'" And then "the castle was demolished from its lowest to its highest stone."

This final statement is a little too sweep [170] ing, yet essentially it is true. All that now remains of Crussol is a single broken tower, to which some minor ruins cling; and a little lower are the ruins of the town—whence the encircling ramparts have been outcast and lie in scattered fragments down the mountain-side to the border of the Rhône.

It was on this very mountain—a couple of thousand years or so earlier in the world's history—that a much pleasanter personage than a battling baron had his home: a good-natured giant of easy morals who was the traditional founder of Valence. Being desirous of founding a town somewhere, and willing—in accordance with the custom of his time—to leave the selection of a site a little to chance, he hurled a javelin from his mountain-top with the cry, "Va lance!": and so gave Valence its name and its beginning, on the eastern bank of the river two miles away, at the spot where his javelin fell. At a much later period the Romans adopted and enlarged the giant's foundation; but nearly every trace of their occupation has disappeared. Indeed, even the ramparts, built only a few hundred years ago by Francis I., [171] have utterly vanished; and the tendency of the town has been so decidedly toward pulling down and building up again that it now wears quite a modern and jauntily youthful air.

Valence was our next stopping-place, and we had a world of work to do there during the hour or so that we remained ashore. Very properly believing that we, being poets, could dedicate their local monuments for them far better than they could do such work for themselves, the excellent people of this town had accumulated a variety of monuments in expectation of our coming; and all of these it was our pleasant duty to start upon their immortal way.

Our reception was nothing short of magnificent. On the suspension bridge which here spans the river half the town was assembled watching for us; and the other half was packed in a solid mass on the bank above the point where our landing was made. The landing-stage was a glorious blaze of tri-colour; and there the Mayor, also gloriously tri-coloured, stood waiting for us in the midst of a guard of honour of four firemen whose brazen helmets shone resplendent in the rays [172] of the scorching sun. A little in the background was the inevitable band; that broke with a crash, at the moment of our landing, into the inevitable "Marseillaise." And then away we all marched for half a mile, up a wide and dusty and desperately hot street, into the heart of the town. The detachment of welcoming townsfolk from the bank closed in around us; and around them, presently, closed in the detachment of welcoming townsfolk from the bridge. We poets (I insist upon being known by the company I was keeping) were deep in the centre of the press. The heat was prodigious. The dust was stifling. But, upheld by a realizing sense of the importance and honour of the duties confided to us, we never wavered in our march.

Our first halt was before a dignified house on which was a flag-surrounded tablet reading: "Dans cette maison est né Général Championnet. L'an MDCCLXII." M. Faure and Sextius Michel made admirable speeches. The band played the "Marseillaise." We cheered and cheered. But what in the world we poets had to do with this military person—who served under the lilies at the siege of [173] Gibraltar that ended so badly in the year 1783, and who did a great deal of very pretty fighting later under the tri-colour—I am sure I do not know! Then on we went, to the quick tap of the drums, the Mayor and the glittering firemen preceding us, to the laying of a corner-stone that really was in our line: that of a monument to the memory of the dramatist Émile Augier. Here, naturally, M. Jules Claretie came to the fore. In the parlance of the Academy, Augier was "his dead man"; and not often does it happen that a finer, a more discriminating, eulogy is pronounced in the Academy by the successor to a vacant chair than was pronounced that hot day in Valence upon Émile Augier by the Director of the Comédie Française. When it was ended, there was added to the contents of the leaden casket a final paper bearing the autographs of the notables of our company; and then the cap-stone, swinging from tackles, was lowered away.

We had the same ceremony over again, ten minutes later, when we laid the corner-stone of the monument to the Comte de Montalivet: who was an eminent citizen and [174] Mayor of Valence, and later was a Minister under the first Napoleon—whom he had met at Madame Colombier's, likely enough, in the days when the young artillery officer was doing fitful garrison-duty in that little town. Again it seemed to me that we poets were not necessarily very closely associated with the matter in hand; but we cheered at the proper places, and made appropriate and well-turned speeches, and contributed a valuable collection of autographs to the lead box in the corner-stone: and did it all with the easily off-hand air of thorough poets of the world. In the matter of the autographs there was near to being a catastrophe. Everything was going at a quick-step— our time being so short—and in the hurry of it all the lead box was closed and the cap-stone was lowered down upon it while yet the autographs remained outside! It was by the merest chance, I fancy, in that bustling confusion, that the mistake happened to be noticed; and I cannot but think—the autographs, with only a few exceptions, being quite illegible—that no great harm would have come had it passed unobserved. However, the omission being [175] discovered, common courtesy to the autographists required that the cap-stone should be raised again and the much-signed paper put where it belonged.

Having thus made what I believe to be a dedicatory record by dedicating three monuments, out of a possible four, in considerably less than an hour, we were cantered away to the Hôtel de Ville to be refreshed and complimented with a "Vin d'honneur." That ceremony came off in the council chamber—a large, stately room—and was impressive. M. le Maire was a tall man, with a cherubic face made broader by wing-like little whiskers. He wore a white cravat, a long frock-coat, appositely black trousers, and a far-reaching white waistcoat over which wandered tranquilly his official tri-coloured scarf. The speech which he addressed to us was of the most flattering. He told us plainly that we were an extraordinarily distinguished company; that our coming to Valence was an event to be remembered long and honourably in the history of the town; that he, personally and officially, was grateful to us; and that, personally and officially, he would have [176] the pleasure of drinking to our very good health. And then (most appropriately by the brass-helmeted firemen) well-warmed champagne was served; and in that cordial beverage, after M. Édouard Lockroy had made answer for us, we pledged each other with an excellent good will.

I am sorry to say that we "scamped" our last monument. To be sure, it was merely a tablet in a house-front setting forth the fact that Émile Augier had been born there; and already Augier had had one of the best speeches of the day. But that was no excuse for us. Actually, we scarcely waited to see the veil of pink paper torn away by a man on a step-ladder before we broke for the boat—and not a speech of any sort was made! Yet they bore us no malice, those brave Valençois. All the way down to the river, under the blaze of the sun, they crowded closely around us—with a well-meant but misapplied friendliness—and breathed what little air was stirring thrice over before it had a chance to get to our lungs. They covered again in a black swarm the bank and the bridge in our honour. Their band, through [177] that last twenty minutes, blared steadfastly the "Marseillaise." From his post upon the landing-stage the cherubic Mayor beamed to us across his nobly tri-coloured stomach a series of parting smiles. The brass-helmeted firemen surrounded him—a little unsteadily, I fancied—smiling too. And as we slipped away from them all, into the rush of the river, they sent after us volley upon volley of cheers. Our breasts thrilled and expanded—it is not always that we poets thus are mounted upon high horses in the sight of all the world—and we cheered back to those discriminating and warm-hearted towns-folk until we fairly were under way down-stream. To the very last the cherubic Mayor, his hat raised, regarded us smilingly. To the very last—rivalling the golden glory of the helmet of Mambrino—the slightly-wavering head-gear of his attendant firemen shot after us golden gleams.

VIII

We drew away into calmer latitudes after leaving that whirlwind of a town. For the [178] time being, our duties as public poets were ended; and there was a sense of restful comfort in knowing that for the moment we were rid of our fame and celebrity, and were free — as the lightest hearted of simple travellers — to enjoy the beauties of the river as it carried us, always at a full gallop, downward toward the sea.

In that tranquil spirit we came, presently, to the leaning Tour-Maudite: and found farther restfulness, after our own varied and too-energetic doings, in looking upon a quiet ruin that had remained soberly in the same place, and under the same sedative curse, for more than three hundred years. It is an architectural curiosity, this Curséd Tower — almost as far out from the perpendicular as is its better-known rival of Pisa; but more impressive in its unnatural crookedness because it stands upon an isolated crag which drops below it sheer to the river in a vast precipice. Anciently, before it went wrong and its curse came upon it, the tower was the keep of the Benedictine nunnery of Soyons. Most ungallantly, in the year 1569, the Huguenots captured the Abbey by assault; and [179] thereupon the Abbess, Louise d'Amauze (poor frightened soul!) hurriedly embraced the Reformed religion — in dread lest, without that concession to the prejudices of the conquerors, still worse might come. Several of her nuns followed her hastily heterodox example; but the mass of them stood stoutly by their faith, and ended by making off with it intact to Valence. I admit that an appearance of improbability is cast upon this tradition by the unhindered departure from the Abbey of the stiff-necked nuns: who thus manifested an open scorn equally of the victorious Huguenots and of the Reformed faith. But, on the other hand, there are the ruins of the Abbey to prove conclusively that it truly was conquered; and there, slanting with a conspicuously unholy slant high up above the ruins, bearing steadfast witness to the wrath of heaven against that heretical Abbess and her heretical followers, is the Curséd Tower!

While the Abbess of Soyons, being still untried by the stress of battle, went sinless upon her still orthodox way, there lived just across the river on the Manor of l'Étoile a sinner of a gayer sort — Diane de Poitiers. [180] The Castle of the Star dates from the fifteenth century; when Louis XI. dwelt there as Governor of Dauphiny and was given lessons in how to be a king. Diane the beautiful—"the most beautiful," as Francis I. gallantly called her—transformed the fortress into a bower, and gave to it (or accepted for it) the appropriately airy name of the Château de Papillon. There she lived long after her butterfly days were over; and in a way—although the Castle of the Butterfly is a silk-factory now—she lives there still: just as another light lady beautiful, Queen Jeanne of Naples, lives on in Provence. To this day her legend is vital in the country-side; and the old people still talk about her as though she were alive among them; and call her always not by her formal title of the Duchesse de Valentinois, but by her love title of "la belle dame de l'Étoile." Of this joyous person's family there is found a ghastly memento at the little town of Lène—a dozen miles down the river, beyond the great iron-works of Le Pouzin. It is the Tour de la Lépreuse: wherein a leper lady of the house of Poitiers was shut up for many years in awful solitude [181] —until at last God in his goodness permitted her to die. I suppose that this story would have pointed something of a moral—instead of presenting only another case of a good moral gone wrong—had Diane herself been that prisoner of loathsome death in life.

But aboard the *Gladiateur* our disposition was to take the world easily and as we found it—since we found it so well disposed toward us—and not to bother our heads a bit about how moral lessons came off. With cities effervescing in our honour, with Mayors attendant upon us hat in hand, with brazen-helmeted firemen playing champagne upon us to stimulate our poetic fires, with *boîtes* and bands exploding in our praise—and all under that soul-expanding sun of the Midi—'tis no wonder that we wore our own bays jauntily and nodded to each other as though to say: "Ah, you see now what it is to be a poet in these latter days!" And we were graciously pleased to accept as a part of the tribute that all the world just then was rendering to us the panorama of mountains and towns and castles that continuously opened before us for the delectation of our souls. [182]

Off to the right, hidden behind the factory-smoke of La Voulte, was the sometime home of Bernard de Ventadour, a troubadour whom the world still loves to honour—quite one of ourselves; off to the left, commanding the valley of the Drôme, were Livron and

Loriol, tough little Huguenot nuts cracked all to pieces (as their fallen ramparts showed) in the religious wars; and a little lower down we came to Cruas: a famous fortified Abbey, surmounted by a superb donjon and set in the midst of a triple-walled town, whereof the Byzantine-Romanesque church is one of the marvels of Southern France. Cruas was founded more than a thousand years ago, in the time of Charlemagne, by the pious Hermengarde, wife of Count Eribert de Vivarais; being a thank-offering to heaven erected on the very spot where that estimable woman and her husband were set upon in the forest by a she-wolf of monstrous size. But the fortified Abbey was a later growth; and was not completed, probably, until the sixteenth century. It was toward the end of that century, certainly, that the Huguenots attacked it—and were beaten off final [183] ly by Abbot Étienne Déodel and his monks, who clapped on armour over their habits and did some very sprightly fighting on its walls.

Below Cruas, around the bend in the river, Rochemaure the Black came into sight: a withered stronghold topping an isolated rock of black basalt six hundred feet above the stream. It is a grewsome place: the ruin of a black nightmare of a basalt-built castle, having below and around it a little black nightmare of a basalt-built town— whereof the desperately steep and crooked streets are paved with black basalt, and are so narrowed by over-hanging houses as to show above them only the merest strip of sky. It is a town to which, by preference, one would go to commit a murder; but 'tis said that its inhabitants are kindly disposed. Only a step beyond it lies Le Teil: a briskly busy little place tucked in at the foot of a lime-stone cliff—town and cliff and the inevitable castle on the cliff-top all shrouded in a murky white cloud, half dust, half vapour, rising from the great buildings in which a famous hydraulic cement is made. Not a desirable [184] abiding place, seemingly; but in cheerful contrast with its lowering neighbour up the stream.

And then, passing beyond a maze of islands—amidst which the river wandered so tortuously that our pilot had behind him a strong tiller-crew in order to carry us through safely—we came to the noble town of Viviers. From afar we saw its tall bell-tower, its beautiful cathedral, its episcopal palace; and as we drew nearer the whole environment of ancient houses and fortifications spread out around those governing points in a great amphitheatre. But what held us most was the gay dash of tri-colour on its bridge, and the crowd there evidently waiting for our coming to manifest toward us their good will. They cheered us and waved their hats and handkerchiefs at us, those poet-lovers, as we neared them; and as we passed beneath the bridge a huge wreath of laurel was swung downward to our deck, and a shower of laurel branches fluttered down upon us through the sunlit air. In all the fourteen centuries since Viviers was founded I am confident that nothing more gracious than this tribute to [185] passing Poetry is recorded in the history of the town.

Naturally, being capable of such an act of nicely discriminating courtesy, Viviers has sound traditions of learning and of gentle blood. In its day it was a great episcopal city: whose bishops maintained an army, struck money, counted princes among their vassals, in set terms defied the power of the King of France — and recognized not the existence of any temporal sovereign until the Third Conrad of Germany enlarged their knowledge of political geography by taking their city by storm. Yet while finely lording it over outsiders, the bishops were brought curiously to their bearings within their own walls. Each of them, in turn, on his way to his installation, found closed against him, as he descended from his mule before it, the door of the cathedral; and the door was not opened until he had sworn there publicly that he would maintain inviolate as he found them the rights and privileges of the chapter and of the town. Moreover, once in each year the men and women of rank of Viviers asserted their right to a part enjoyment of the [186] ecclesiastical benefices by putting on copes and mitres and occupying with the canons the cathedral stalls.

The line of one hundred and thirty bishops who in succession reigned here ended — a century back, in the time of the Revolution — in a veritable lurid flame; yet with, I think, a touch of agonized human nature too. The church historian can see only the diabolical side of the situation; and in a horror-struck way tells how that last Bishop, "being overcome by the devil, abjured the episcopacy; with his own hands destroyed the insignia of his sacred office; and thereafter gave himself up to a blasphemous attack upon the holy religion of which he had been for a long while one of the most worthy ministers."

It certainly is true that the devil had things largely his own way about that time here in France; but it does not necessarily follow that in this particular matter the devil directly had a hand. To my mind a simpler and more natural explanation presents itself: That the iconoclastic Bishop was a weak brother who had suffered himself to be forced into a calling for which he had no vocation, [187] and into an apparent championship of a faith with which his inmost convictions were at war; that for years and years the struggle between the inward man and the outward Bishop had gone on unceasingly and hopelessly, until—as well enough might happen to one strong enough to resent yet not strong enough to overcome restraint—the galling irksomeness of such a double life had brought madness near; and that madness did actually come when the chains of a life and of a faith alike intolerable suddenly were fused in the fierce heat of the Revolution and fell away.

IX

Below Viviers the Rhône breaks out from its broad upper valley into its broader lower valley through the Defile of Donzère. Here the foothills of the Alps and the foothills of the Cévennes come together, and behind this natural dam there must have been anciently a great lake which extended to the northward of where now is Valence. The Defile is a veritable cañon that would be quite [188] in place in the Sierra Madre. On each side of the sharply-narrowed river the walls of rock rise sheer to a height of two hundred feet. The rush of the water is tumultuous. In mid-stream, surrounded by eddies and whirling waves, is the Roche-des-Anglais—against which the boat of a luckless party of English travellers struck and was shattered a hundred years ago. Indeed, so dangerous was this passage held to be of old—when faith was stronger and boats were weaker than in our day of skepticism and compound-engines—that it was customary to tie-up at the head of the Defile and pray for grace to come through it safely; and sincerely faithful travellers tied-up again when the passage was ended to offer a service of grateful praise. But nowadays they clap five men on the tiller and put on more steam—and the practical result is the same.

The cliffs bordering the cañon, being of a crumbling nature, are known as the Maraniousques; but usually are called by the Rhône boatmen the Monkey Rocks—because of the monkeys who dwelt in them in legendary times and stoned from their heights the pass [189] ing travellers. It was a long while ago that the monkeys were in possession—in the time immediately succeeding the Deluge. During the subsidence of the waters it seems that the Ark made fast there for the night, just before laying a course for Ararat; and the monkey and his wife—desperately bored by their long cooping-up among so many uncongenial animals—took advantage of their opportunity to pry a couple of tiles off the roof and get away. The tradition hints that Noah had been drinking; at any rate, their absence was not noticed, and the Ark went on without them the next day. By the time that the Deluge fairly was ended, and the Rhône reopened to normal navigation, a large monkey family was established on the Maraniousques; and the monkeys thenceforward illogically revenged themselves upon Noah's descendants by stoning everybody who came along.

Later, the ill-tempered monkeys were succeeded by more ill-tempered men. In the fighting times the Defile of Donzère was a famous place in which to bring armies to a stand. Fortifications upon the cliffs entirely [190] commanded the river; and at the lower end of the Defile the castle and the walled town of Donzère, capping a defiant little hill-top, commanded both the river and the plain. Even the most fire-eating of captains were apt to stop and think a little before venturing into the Defile in those days.

All of those perils are ended now. The dangers of the river are so shorn by steam that the shooting of the cañon rapids yields only a pleasurable excitement, that is increased by the extraordinary wild beauty of that savage bit of nature in the midst of a long-tamed land; and the ramparts and the castle of Donzère, having become invitingly picturesque ruins, are as placable remnants of belligerency as are to be found anywhere in the world. Indeed, as we saw them—with the afternoon sunlight slanting down in a way to bring out delectably the warm greys and yellows of the stone-work and to produce the most entrancing effects of light-and-shade—it was not easy to believe that people had been killing each other all over them not so very long ago.

THE DEFILE OF DONZÈRE

Having escaped from the Defile of Donzère, [191] the river wanders away restfully into a wilderness of islands—a maze so unexplored and so unexplorable that otters still make their home in it, and through the thick foliage poke out their snub noses at passing boatmen now and then. Thence onward for a long way islands are plentiful—past Pierrelatte, and Bourg-Saint-Andéol, (a very ancient and highly Roman flavoured town), and the confluence of the Rhône and the Ardèche—to the still larger archipelago across which the Bridge Building Brothers, with God himself helping them, built the Pont-Saint-Esprit.

Modern engineers—possibly exalting their own craft at the expense of that of the architects—declare that this bridge was the greatest piece of structural work of the Middle Ages; certainly it was the greatest work of the Frères Pontifes: that most practical of brotherhoods which, curiously anticipating one phase of modern doctrine, paid less attention to faith than to works and gave itself simply to ministering to the material welfare of mankind. In the making of it they spent near half a century. From the year 1265 steadily onward until the year 1307 the [192] Brothers labored: and then the bridge was finished—a half-mile miracle in stone. In view of the extraordinary difficulties which the engineer in charge of the work overcame—founding piers in bad holding-ground and in the thick of that tremendous current, with the work broken off short by the frequent floods and during the long season of high water in the spring—it is not surprising that the miracle theory was adopted to explain his eventual victory. Nor is it surprising that the popular conviction presently began to sustain itself by crystalizing into a definite legend—based upon the recorded fact that the Brothers worked under the vocation of the Holy Spirit—to the effect that the Spirit of God, taking human form, was the designer of the fabric and the actual director under whose guidance the work went on. And so the genesis of the bridge was accounted for satisfactorily; and so it came by its holy name.

Personally, I like miracles; and this miracle is all the more patent, I think, now that the bridge has been in commission for almost six hundred years and still is entirely ser [193] viceable. Yet while its piers and arches, its essential parts, remain nearly as the Brothers built them, the bridge has undergone such modifications in the course of the past century—in order to fit it to the needs of modern traffic—that its picturesqueness has been destroyed. The chapel of St. Nicholas upon one of its piers, and the tower at its centre, were razed about the end of the last century; a little later the fortified approaches were removed; in the year 1854, to provide for the increasing river navigation, the first two arches from the right bank were replaced by a single iron arch of two hundred feet span over the main channel; and in the year 1860 the entire superstructure on the north side, with a part of the superstructure on the south side, was torn down—and in place of the old narrow roadway, with turnouts on each pier, there was built a roadway uniformly twenty-two feet wide. In a sentimental way, of course, these radical changes are to be regretted; but I am sure that the good Brothers, could they have been consulted in the premises, would have been the first to sanction them. For they were not sentimentalists, the Broth [194] ers; they were practical to the last degree. What they wanted was that their bridge, living up to their own concept of duty, should do the greatest amount of good to the greatest number of men.

Almost as we came out from beneath that monument to practical Christianity, we saw over on the left bank two monuments to the theoretical Christianity of three hundred years ago: the grisly ruins of Mornas and Montdragon—each on a hill dark green with a thick growth of *chêne vert*, and each having about it (not wholly because of its dark setting, I fancied) a darkly sinister air. In truth, the story of Mornas is sombre enough to blacken not merely a brace of hill-tops but a whole neighbourhood. In the early summer of the year 1565, a day or two before the Fête-Dieu, the Papists surprised and seized the town and castle and put the entire Huguenot garrison to the sword. Then, as now, it was the custom in honour of the Fête-Dieu to adorn the house-fronts with garlands and draperies; and by way of variant upon this pretty custom "certain of the conquerors, more fanatical than the rest, flayed the dead Huguenots [195] and draped their houses bravely with Protestant skins." Thereupon the Baron des Adrets, the Huguenot commander in that region, sent one of his lieutenants, Dupuy-Montbrun, to avenge that deviltry. At the end of a three-days' siege Mornas was conquered again, and then came the vengeance: "for which the castle of Mornas, whereof the battlements overhung a precipice falling sheer two hundred feet to broken rocks below, offered great advantages." In a grave and orderly fashion, the survivors of the conquered garrison were as-sembled in the castle court-yard; were taken in orderly squads of ten up to the battlements; and thence were thrust over into that awful depth. And so the account was squared.

It is instructive to note that des Adrets, who ordered the venge-ance on Mornas, a little later abjured the Reformed religion and became a Papist; and that Dupuy-Montbrun, who carried out his orders and who succeeded him upon his recantation in the com-mand of the Protestant army, but a little while before had re-nounced Papacy to become a Huguenot. So the leaders, the worst of [196] them, shifted from side to side as they happened to be swayed by pay or policy; and to such creatures of no real faith were due the direst of the atrocities of those hideous times. But the Huguenots of the rank and file were of another sort. Their singleness and sincerity in their fight for their faith were beyond question. They died for it willingly. Failing the happiness of death, yet being conquered, they still held fast to it. In the end, rather than relinquish it, they unhesi-tatingly elected — at a stroke giving up country, rank, fortune — to be outcast from France.

For me the history of those desperate wars has a very vital inter-est: for my own ancestors took the share in them that was becoming to faithful gentlemen vowed to the Reform, and I owe my American birthright to the honourable fact that they fought on the losing side. As I myself am endowed with a fair allowance of stubbornness, and with a strong distaste to taking my opinions at second hand, I certainly should have been with my kinsfolk in that fight had I lived in their day; and since my destiny was theirs [197] to determine I am strongly grateful to them for having shaped it so well.

X

But I was glad when Mornas, vivid with such bitter memories, dropped out of sight astern. Sleeping dogs of so evil a sort very well may lie; though it is difficult not to waken a few of them when they lie so thickly as here in the Rhône Valley, where almost every town and castle has a chapter of nightmare horrors all its own.

Even Châteauneuf-du-Pape—which we saw a half hour later off to the eastward, rising from a little hill-top and thence overlooking the wide vineyard-covered valley—came to its present ruin at the hands of des Adrets; who, having captured and fired it, left standing only its tall square tower and some fragments of its walls. This was an unfairly lurid ending for a castle which actually came into existence for gentle purposes and was not steeped to its very battlements in crime; for Châteauneuf was built purely [198] as a pleasure-place, to which the Popes—when weary with ruling the world and bored by their strait-laced duties as Saint Peter's earthly representatives—might come from Avignon with a few choice kindred spirits and refreshingly kick up their heels. As even in Avignon, in those days, the Popes and cardinals did not keep their heels any too fast to the ground, it is an inferential certainty that the kicking up at Châteauneuf must have been rather prodigiously high; but the people of the Middle Ages were too stout of stomach to be easily scandalized, and the Pope's responsibilities in the premises were all the lighter because the doctrine of his personal infallibility had not then been formulated officially. And so things went along comfortably in a cheerfully reprehensible way.

It was in those easy-going days that the vineyards were planted, on the slopes below the castle, which were destined to make the name of Châteauneuf-du-Pape famous the toping world over long after the New Castle should be an old ruin and the Avignon Popes a legend of the past. Only within the present generation did those precious vines perish, [199] when the phylloxera began among them its deadly work in France; and even yet may be found, tucked away here and there in the favoured cellars of Provence and Languedoc, a few dust-covered bottles of their rich vintage: which has for its distinguishing taste a sublimated spiciness due to the alternate dalliance of the bees with the grape-blossoms and with the blossoms of the wild thyme. It is a wine of poets, this bee-kissed Châteauneuf, and its noblest association is not with the Popes who gave their name to it but with the seven poets—Mistral, Roumanille, Aubanel, Matthieu, Brunet, Giéra, Tavan—whose chosen drink it was in those glorious days when they all were young together and were founding the Félibrige: the society that was to restore the golden age of the Troubadours and, incidentally, to decentralize France. One of the sweetest and gentlest of the seven, Anselme Matthieu, was born here at Châteauneuf; and here, with a tender love-song upon his lips, only the other day he died. The vineyards have been replanted, and in the fulness of time may come to their glory again; but the greater glories of Château [200] neuf—which belonged to it once because of its Popes, and again because of its sweet-souled Poet— must be only memories forevermore.

THE ROU-MANILLE MONUMENT

The castles over on the right bank, Montfaucon and Roquemaure, are of the normal painful sort again. Roquemaure is a crooked, narrow, up-and-down old dirty town, where old customs and old costumes and old forms of speech still live on; and, also, its people have a very pretty taste in the twisting and perverting of historic fact into picturesque tradition—as is shown by the way in which they have rearranged the unpleasant details of the death of Pope Clement V. into a bit of melodramatic moral decoration for their own town. Their ingeniously compiled legend runs in this wise: Clement's death in the castle of Roquemaure occurred while he was on his way homeward from the Council of Vienne; where—keeping with the King the bargain which had won for him the Papal throne—he had abolished the Order of the Templars and had condemned their Grand Master, Jacques de Molay, to be burned alive. When that sentence was passed, the Grand [201] Master, in turn, had passed sentence of death upon the Pope: declaring that within forty days they should appear together, in the spirit, to try again that cause misjudged on earth before the Throne of God. And the forty days were near ended when Pope Clement came to Roquemaure—with the death-grip already so strong upon him that even the little farther journey to Avignon was impossible, and he could but lay him down there and die. While yet the breath scarce was out of his body, his servants fell to fighting over his belongings with a brutal fierceness: in the midst of which fray a lighted torch fell among and fired the hangings of the bed whereon lay the dead Pope—and before any of the pillagers would give the rest an advantage by stopping in their foul work to extinguish the flames his body was half-consumed. And so was Clement burned in death even as the Grand Master had been burned in life; and so was executed upon him the Grand Master's summons to appear before the Judgment Seat on high!

It is interesting to note that this tradition [202] does very little violence to the individual facts of the case, and yet rearranges them in such a fashion that they are at sixes and sevens with the truth as a whole. When, in my lighter youth, I entered upon what I fancied was antiquarian research I was hot for the alluring theory that oral tradition is a surer preserver of historic fact than is written record; and as I was not concerned with antiquities of a sort upon which my pretty borrowed theory could be tested I got along with it very well. But I am glad now to cite this capital instance in controversion of my youthful second-hand belief—because it entirely accords with my more mature conviction that oral tradition, save as a tenacious preserver of place-names, is not to be trusted at all. And as unsupported written record rarely is to be trusted either, it would seem that a certain amount of reason was at the root of King David's hasty generalization as to the untruthfulness of mankind.

The day was nearly ended as we passed that town with a stolen moral history: and so swept onward, in and out among the islands, [203] toward Avignon. Already the sun had fallen below the crest of the Cévennes; leaving behind him in the sky a liquid glory, and still sending far above us long level beams which gilded radiantly—far off to the eastward—the heights of Mont-Ventour. But we, deep in the deep valley, threaded our swift way among the islands in a soft twilight which gently ebbed to night.

And then, as the dusk deepened to the westward, there came slowly into the eastern heavens a pale lustre that grew brighter and yet brighter until, all in a moment, up over the Alpilles flashed the full moon—and there before us, almost above us, the Rocher-des-Doms and the Pope's Palace and the ramparts of Avignon stood out blackly against the moon-bright sky. So sudden was this ending to our journey that there was a wonder among us that the end had come!

All the Félibres of Avignon were at the water-side to cheer us welcome as the *Gladiateur,* with reversed engines, hung against the current above the bridge of Saint-Bénézet and slowly drew in to the bank. Our answer [204] ing cheers went forth to them through the darkness, and a stave or two of "La Coupe" was sung, and there was a mighty clapping of hands. And then the gang-plank was set ashore, and instantly beside it—standing in the glare of a great lantern—we saw our Capoulié, the head of all the Félibrige, Félix Gras, waiting for us, his subjects and his brethren, with outstretched hands. From him came also, a little later, our official welcome: when we all were assembled for a *ponch d'honneur* at the Hôtel du Louvre—in the great vaulted chamber that once served the Templars as a refectory, and that has been the banquet-hall of the Félibrige ever since this later and not less honorable Order was founded, almost forty years ago.

AVIGNON

Not until those formalities were ended could we of America get away to receive the personal welcome to which through all that day we had been looking forward with a warm eagerness—yet also sorrowing: because we knew that among the welcoming voices there would be a silence, and that a face would be missing from among those we loved. Roumanille was dead; and in meet [205] ing again in Avignon those who had been closest and dearest to him, and who to us were close and dear, there was heartache with our joy.

Saint-Remy-de-Provence,
August, 1894.

[209]

The Comédie Française
at Orange

I

After a lapse of nearly fifteen centuries, the Roman theatre at Orange—founded in the time of Marcus Aurelius and abandoned, two hundred years later, when the Northern barbarians overran the land—seems destined to arise reanimate from its ruins and to be the scene of periodic performances by the Comédie Française: the first dramatic company of Europe playing on the noblest stage in the world. During the past five-and-twenty years various attempts have been made to compass this happy end. Now—as the result of the representations of "Œdipus" and "Antigone" at Orange, under government patronage and by the leading actors of the National Theatre—these spasmodic efforts have crystallized into a steadfast endeavour which promises to [210] restore and to repeople that long-abandoned stage. [4]

GENERAL VIEW OF THE THEATRE

If they know about it—over there in the Shades—I am sure that no one rejoices more sincerely over this revival than do the Romans by whom the theatre at Orange was built, and from whom it has come down to us as one of the many proofs of their strong affection for that portion of their empire which now is the south-east corner of France. To them this region, although ultimately included in the larger Narbonensis, always was simply Provincia—*the* Province: a distinguishing indistinction which exalted it above all the other dependencies of Rome. Constantine, indeed, was for fixing the very seat of the Empire here; and he did build, and for a time live in, the palace at Arles of which a stately fragment still remains. Unluckily for the world of later periods, he was [211] lured away from the banks of the Rhône by the charms of the Bosporus—and so, without knowing it, opened the Eastern Question: that ever since has been fought over, and that still demands for its right answering at least one more general European war.

Thus greatly loving their Province, the Romans gladly poured out their treasure in adding to its natural beauties the adornments of art. Scattered through this region—through the Provence of to-day, and, over on the other side of the Rhône, through Languedoc—are the remnants of their magnificent creations: the Pont-du-Gard; the arena, and the baths, and the Tour-Magne, and the beautiful Maison-Carrée, at Nîmes; at Arles the arena, the palace of Constantine, and the wreck of the once exquisite theatre; the baths at Aix; the triumphal arches at Orange and Carpentras; the partly ruined but more perfectly graceful arch, and the charming monument, here at Saint-Remy—all these relics of Roman splendour, with many others which I have not named, still testify to Roman affection for this enchanting land.

The theatre at Orange—the Arausio of Ro [212] man times, colonized by the veterans of the Second Legion—was not the best of these many noble edifices. Decidedly, the good fortune that has preserved so large a part of it would have been better bestowed upon the far more beautiful, because more purely Grecian, theatre at Arles: which the blessed Saint Hilary and the priest Cyril of holy memory fell afoul of in the fifth century and destroyed because of its inherent idolatrous wickedness, and then used as raw material for their well-meant but injudicious church-building. But the Orange theatre—having as its only extant rival that at Pompeii—has the distinction of being the most nearly perfect Roman theatre surviving until our day; and, setting aside comparisons with things nonexistent, it is one of the most majestic structures to be found in the whole of France. Louis XIV., who styled it "the most magnificent wall of my kingdom," placed it first of all.

The unknown architect who wrought this great work—traversing the Roman custom of erecting a complete building on level ground—followed the Grecian custom of hollowing [213] out a hillside and of facing the open cutting with a structure of masonry: which completed the tiers of seats cut in the living rock; provided in its main body the postscenium, and in its wings the dressing-rooms; and, rising in front to a level with the colonnade which crowned and surrounded the auditorium, made at once the outer façade and the rear wall of the stage. [5] The dominant characteristic of the building—a great parallelogram jutting out from the hill-side into the very heart of the town—is its powerful mass. The enormous façade, built of great blocks of stone, is severely simple: a stony height—the present bareness of which formerly was a little relieved by the vast wooden portico that extended along the entire front— based upon a cornice surmounting open Tuscan arches and broken only by a few strong lines. The essential principle of the whole is stability. It is the Roman style with all its good qualities exaggerated. Elegance is re [214] placed by a heavy grandeur; purity by strength.

The auditorium as originally constructed—save for the graceful colonnade which surmounted its enclosing wall, and for the ornamentation which certainly was bestowed upon the rear wall of the stage and probably upon the facing-wall of the first tier of seats— was as severe as the façade: simply bare tiers of stone benches, divided into three distinct stages, rising steplike one above another in a great semi-circle. But when the theatre was filled with an eager multitude its bareness disappeared; and its brilliant lowest division—where sat the nobles clad in purple-bordered white robes: a long sweep of white dashed with strong colour—fitly brought the auditorium into harmony with the splendour of the permanent setting of the stage.

It was there, on the wall rising at the back of the stage and on the walls rising at its sides, that decoration mainly was bestowed; and there it was bestowed lavishly. Following the Grecian tradition (though in the Grecian theatre the sides of the stage were open gratings) that permanent set repre [215] sented very magnificently— being, indeed, a reality—a royal palace, or, on occasion, a temple: a façade broken by richly carved marble cornices supported by marble columns and pilasters; its flat surfaces covered with brilliantly coloured mosaics, and having above its five portals [6] arched alcoves in which were statues: that over the royal portal, the *aula regia*, being a great statue of the Emperor or of a god.

Extending across the whole front of this [216] wall, entirely filling the space between the wings, was the stage. Ninety feet above it, also filling the space between the wings, was a wooden roof (long since destroyed) which flared upward and outward: at once adding to the acoustic properties of the building and protecting the stage from rain. Still farther to strengthen the acoustic effect, two curved walls — lateral sounding-boards — projected from the rear of the stage and partly embraced the space upon which the action of the play usually went on.

I shall not enter into the vexed question of scenery. It is sufficient to say that this permanent set, in regard to which there can be no dispute — a palace, that also would serve as a temple — made an entirely harmonious framework for most of the plays which were presented here. Indeed, a more fitting or a more impressive setting could not have been devised for the majority of the tragedies of that time: which were filled with a solemn grandeur, and which had for their chief personages priests or kings. Above all, the dignity of this magnificent permanent scene was in keeping with the devotional solemnity of [217] the early theatre: when an inaugural sacrifice was celebrated upon an altar standing in front of the stage, and when the play itself was in the nature of a religious rite.

II

Certainly for two centuries, possibly for a longer period, the people of Arausio maintained and enjoyed their theatre. The beautiful little city of which it was a part was altogether charming: abounding in comforts and luxuries and rich in works of art. From the hill-top where now stands the statue of the Virgin was to be seen in those days a miniature Rome. Directly at the base of the hill was the theatre, and beyond it were the circus and the baths; to the left, the Coliseum; to the right, the Field of Mars; in front — just within the enclosing ramparts, serving as the chief entrance to the town — the noble triumphal arch that remains almost perfect even until this present day. Only the theatre and the arch are left now; but the vanished elegance of it all is testified to by the frag [218] ments of carved walls and of mosaic pavements which still continue to be unearthed from time to time. Surrounding that opulent little city were farms and vineyards and olive-orchards — a gentle wilderness interset with garden-hidden villas whereto the citizens retired to take their ease; and more widely about it was the broad Rhône Valley, then as now a rich store-house of corn and wine and oil.

No wonder that the lean barbarians of the North came down in hungry hordes and seized upon that fatness as Roman strength decayed; and no wonder, being barbarians, that the invaders wrecked much of the beauty which they could neither use nor understand. After the second German invasion, in the year 406 of our era, there was little left in Gaul of Roman civilization; and after the coming of the Visigoths, four years later, Roman civilization was at an end.

Yet during that period of disintegration the theatre was not injured materially; and it actually remained almost intact—although variously misused and perverted—nearly down to our own day. The Lords of Baux, [219] in the twelfth century, made the building the outguard of their fortress on the hill-top in its rear; and from their time onward little dwellings were erected within it—the creation of which nibbled away its magnificent substance to be used in the making of pygmy walls. But the actual wholesale destruction of the interior did not begin until the year 1622: when Prince Maurice of Nassau and Orange, in manner most unprincely, used the building as a quarry from which to draw material for the system of fortifications devised for his little capital by his Dutch engineers. And this piece of vandalism was as useless as it was iniquitous. Only half a century later—during the temporary occupation of Orange by the French—Prince Maurice's fortifications, built of such precious material, were razed.

In later times quarrying was carried on in the theatre on a smaller scale; but, practically, all that this most outrageous Prince left standing of it still stands: the majestic façade, together with the rooms in the rear of the stage; the huge wings, which look like, and have done duty as, the towers of a feu [220] dal fortress; the major portion of the side walls; most of the substructure, and even a little of the superstructure, of the tiers which completed the semi-circles of seats hollowed out of the hill-side; and above these the broken and weathered remains of the higher tiers cut in the living rock. But the colonnade which crowned the enclosing walls of the auditorium is gone, and many of the upper courses of the walls with it; the stage is gone; the wall at the rear of the stage, seamed and scarred, retains only a few fragments of the columns and pilasters and cornices and mosaics which once made it beautiful; the carvings and sculptures have disappeared; the royal portal, once so magnificent, is but a jagged gap in the masonry; the niche above it, once a fit resting place for a god's image, is shapeless and bare. And until the work of restoration began the whole interior was infested with mean little dwellings which choked it like offensive weeds—while rain and frost steadily were eating into the unprotected masonry and hastening the general decay. [221]

III

This was the theatre's evil condition when, happily, the architect Auguste Caristie, vice-president of the commission charged with the conservation of historical monuments, came down to Orange early in the nineteenth century—and immediately was filled with an enthusiastic determination that the stately building should be purified and restored. The theatre became with him a passion; yet a steadfast passion which continued through more than a quarter of a century. He studied it practically on the ground and theoretically in the cabinet; and as the result of his patient researches he produced his great monograph upon it (published in a sumptuous folio at the charges of the French Government) which won for him a medal of the first class at the Salon of 1855. In this work he reëstablished the building substantially as the Roman architect created it; and so provided the plan in accordance with which the present architect in charge, M. [222] Formigé—working in the same loving and faithful spirit—is making the restoration in stone. Most righteously, as a principal feature of the ceremonies of August, 1894, a bust of Auguste Caristie was set up in Orange close by the theatre which owes its saving and its restoration to the strong purpose of his strong heart.

And then came another enthusiast—they are useful in the world, these enthusiasts—who took up the work at the point where Caristie had laid it down. This was the young editor of the *Revue Méridionale*, Fernand Michel—more widely known by his pseudonym of "Antony Réal." By a lucky calamity—the great inundation of the

Rhône in the year 1840—Michel was detained for a while in Orange: and so was enabled to give to the theatre more than the ordinary tourist's passing glance. By that time, the interior of the building had been cleared and its noble proportions fully were revealed; and as the result of his first long morning's visit he became, as Caristie had become before him, fairly infatuated with it.

For my part, I am disposed to believe that [223] a bit of Roman enchantment still lingers in those ancient walls; that the old gods who presided over their creation—and who continue to live on very comfortably, though a little shyly and in a quiet way, here in the south of France—have still an alluring power over those of us who, being at odds with existing dispensations, are open to their genial influences. But without discussing this side issue, it is enough to say that Michel—lightly taking up what proved to be the resolute work of half a lifetime—then and there vowed himself to the task of restoring and reanimating that ruined and long-silent stage.

For more than twenty years he laboured without arriving at any tangible result; and the third decade of his propaganda almost was ended when at last, in August, 1869, his dream was made a reality and the spell of silence was broken by the presentation of Méhul's "Joseph" at Orange. And the crowning of his happiness came when, the opera ended, his own ode composed for the occasion, "Les Triomphateurs"—set to music by Imbert—echoed in the ancient theatre, and the audience of more than seven thou [224] sand burst into enthusiastic cheering over the victory that he had won. Truly, to be the hero of such a triumph was worth the work of nine-and-twenty years.

Even through the dismal time of the German war no time was lost. M. Michel and his enthusiastic colabourers—prominent among them being "Antony Réal, *fils*," upon whom has descended worthily his father's mantle—cared for the material preservation of the building; and succeeded so well in keeping alive a popular interest in their work that they were able to arrange for yet another dramatic festival at Orange in August, 1874. Both grand and light opera were given. On the first evening "Norma" was sung; on the second, "Le Chalet" and "Galatée." To the presentation of these widely differing works attached a curious importance, in that they brought into strong relief an interesting phase of the theatre's psychology: its absolute intolerance of small things. "Norma" was received with a genuine furore; the two pretty little operas practically were failures. The audience, profoundly stirred by the graver work, seemed to understand instinctively [225] that so majestic a setting was suited only to dramas inspired by the noblest passions and dealing with the noblest themes.

During the ensuing twelve years there was no dramatic performance in the theatre; but in this interval there was a performance of another sort (in April, 1877) which in its way was very beautiful. M. Michel's thrilling "Salute to Provence" was sung by a great chorus with orchestral accompaniment; and sung, in accord with ancient custom—wherein was the peculiar and especial charm of it—at the decline of day. The singers sang in the waning sunlight, which emphasized and enlarged the grandeur of their surroundings: and then all ended, as the music and the daylight together died away.

IV

In August, 1886, a venture was made at Orange the like of which rarely has been made in France in modern times: a new French play demanding positive and strong recognition, the magnificent "Empereur d'Arles," [226] by the Avignon poet Alexis Mouzin, was given its first presentation in the Orange theatre—in the provinces—instead of being first produced on the Paris stage. In direct defiance of the modern French canons of centralization, the great audience was brought together not to ratify opinions formulated by Parisian critics but to express its own opinion at first hand. Silvain, of the Comédie Française, was the *Maximien*; Madame Caristie-Martel, of the Odéon (a grand-daughter of Caristie the architect who saved the theatre from ruin), was the *Minervine*. The support was strong. The stately tragedy—vividly contrasting the tyranny and darkness of pagan Rome with the spirit of light and freedom arising in Christian Gaul—was in perfect keeping with its stately frame. The play went on in a whirl of enthusiastic approval to a triumphant end. There was no question of ratifying the opinion of Parisian critics: those Southerners formed and delivered an opinion of their own. In other words, the defiance of conventions was an artistic victory, a decentralizing success.

Then it was that the Félibres—the poets [227] of Languedoc and of Provence who for forty years have been combating the Parisian attempt to focus in Paris the whole of France—perceived how the Orange theatre could be made to advance their anti-centralizing principles, and so took a hand in its fortunes: with the avowed intention of establishing outside of Paris a national theatre wherein should be given in summer dramatic festivals of the highest class. With the Félibres to attempt is to accomplish; and to their efforts was due the presentation at Orange in August 1888, of the "Œdipus" of Sophocles and Rossini's "Moses"—with Mounet-Sully and Boudouresque in the respective title-rôles. The members of the two Félibrien societies of Paris, the Félibrige and the Cigaliers, were present in force at the performances—so timed as to be a part of their customary biennial summer festival in the Midi—and their command of the Paris newspapers (whereof the high places largely are filled by these brave writers of the South) enabled them to make all Paris and all France ring with their account of the beauty of the Orange spectacle. [228]

Out of their enthusiasm came practical results. A national interest in the theatre was aroused; and so strong an interest that the deputy from the Department of the Drôme—M. Maurice Faure, a man of letters who finds time to be also a statesman—brought to a successful issue his long-sustained effort to obtain from the government a grant of funds to be used not merely for the preservation of the building, but toward its restoration. Thanks to his strong presentation of the case, forty thousand francs was appropriated for the beginning of the work: a sum that has sufficed to pay for the rebuilding of twenty of the tiers. And thus, at last, a substantial beginning was made in the recreation of the majestic edifice; and more than a beginning was made in the realization of the Félibrien project for establishing a national theatre in provincial France.

The festival of last August—again promoted by the Félibres, and mainly organized by M. Jules Claretie, the Director of the Comédie Française—was held, therefore, in celebration of specific achievement; and in two other important particulars it differed from [229] all other modern festivals at Orange. First, it was directly under government patronage—M. Leygues, minister of public instruction and the fine arts, bringing two other cabinet ministers with him, having come down from Paris expressly to preside over it; and, secondly, its brilliantly successful organization and accomplishment under such high auspices have gone far toward creating a positive national demand for a realization of the Félibrien dream: that the theatre, again perfect, shall become the home of the highest dramatic art, and a place of periodic pilgrimage, biennial or even annual, for the whole of the art-loving world.

I am disposed to regard myself as more than usually fortunate in that I was able to be a part of that most brilliant festival, and I am deeply grateful to my Félibrien brethren to whom I owe my share in it. With an excellent thoughtfulness they sent me early word of what was forward among them, and so enabled me to get from New York to Paris in time to go down with the Félibres and the Cigaliers by train to Lyons, and thence—as blithe a boat-load of poets as ever went light- [230] heartedly afloat—on southward to Avignon on the galloping current of the Rhône.

V

Avignon was crowded with dignitaries and personages: M. Leygues, who was to preside over the festival; the ministers of justice and of public works, who were to increase its official dignity; artistic and literary people without end. Of these last—who also, in a way, were first, since to them the whole was due—our special boat from Lyons had brought a gay contingent three hundred strong. With it all, the City of the Popes fairly buzzed like a hive of poetic bees got astray from Hymettus Hill.

From Avignon to Orange the distance is less than eighteen miles, not at all too far for driving; and the intervening country is so rich and so beautiful as to conform in all essentials—save in its commendable freedom from serpents—to the biblical description of Paradise. Therefore, following our own wishes and the advice of several poets—they [231] all are poets down there—we decided to drive to the play rather than to expose ourselves to the rigours of the local railway service: the abject collapse of which, under the strain of handling twelve or fifteen hundred people, the poets truthfully prophesied.

It was five in the afternoon when we got away from Avignon. A mistral—the north wind that is the winter bane and summer blessing of Provence—was blowing briskly; the sun was shining; the crowded Cours de la République was gay with flags and banners and streamers, and with festoons of coloured lanterns which later would be festoons of coloured fire. We passed between the towers of the gateway, left the ramparts behind us, and went onward over the perfect road. Plane-trees arched above us; on each side of the road were little villas deep-set in gardens and bearing upon their stone gate-posts the names of saints. As we increased our distance from the city we came to market-gardens, and then to vineyards, olive-orchards, farms. Rows of bright-green poplars and of dark-green cypress—set up as shields against the mistral—made formal lines across the [232] landscape from east to west. The hedges on the lee-side of the road were white with dust—a lace-like effect, curious and beautiful. Above them, and between the trees, we caught glimpses of Mont Ventour—already beginning to glow like a great opal in the nearly level sun-rays. Old women and children stood in the gateways staring wonderingly at the long procession of vehicles, of which our carriage was a part, all obviously filled with pleasure-seekers and all inexplicable. Pretty girls, without stopping to won-der, accepted with satisfaction so joyous an outburst of merrymak-ing and unhesitatingly gave us their smiles.

We crossed the little river Ouvèze, and as we mounted from it to the northward the tower of the ruined Châteauneuf-du-Pape came into view. A new key was struck in the landscape. The broad white road ran through a brown solitude: a level upland broken into fields of sun-browned stubble and of grey-brown olive-orchards; and then, farther on, through a high desolate plain tufted with sage-brush, whence we had outlook to wide horizons far away. Off to the eastward, cutting against [233] the darkening sky, was the curious row of sharp peaks called the Rat's Teeth. All the range of the Alpilles was taking on a deeper grey. Purple undertones were be-ginning to soften the opalescent fire of Mont Ventour.

Presently the road dipped over the edge of the plain and began a descent, in a perfectly straight line but by a very easy grade, of more than a mile. Here were rows of plane-trees again, which, being of no great age and not meeting over the road, were most noticeable as emphasizing the perspective. And from the crest of this acclivity— down the long dip in the land, at the end of the loom of grey-white road lying shadowy between the perspective lines of trees—we saw rising in sombre mass against the purple haze of sunset, dominating the little city nestled at its base and even dwarfing the mountain at its back, the huge fabric of the theatre.

Dusk had fallen as we drove into Orange—thronged with men and beasts like a Noah's ark. All the streets were alive with people; and streams of vehicles of all sorts were pouring in from the four quarters of the compass and discharging their cargoes on [234] the public squares to a loud buzzing accompaniment of vigorous talk— much in the way that the ark people, thankful to get ashore again, must have come buzzing out on Ararat.

I am sorry to say that the handling of a small part of this crowd by the railway people, and of the whole of it by the local manage- ment, was deplorably bad. The trains were inadequate and irregu- lar; the great mistake was made of opening only three of the many entrances to the theatre; and the artistic error was committed (against the protest of M. Mounet-Sully, who earnestly desired to maintain the traditions of the Greek theatre by reserving the orches- tra for the evolutions of the chorus) of filling the orchestra with chairs: with the result that these so-called first-class seats—being all on the same level, and that level four feet lower than the stage— were at once the highest-priced and the worst seats in the building. Decidedly the best seats, both for seeing and hearing, were those of the so-called second class—the newly erected tiers of stone. But so excellent are the acoustic properties of the theatre, even now when the stage is roofless, that [235] in the highest tier of the third-class seats (temporary wooden benches filling the space not yet rebuilt in stone in the upper third of the auditorium) all the well-trained and well-managed voices could be clearly heard.

Naturally, the third-class seats were the most in demand; and from the moment that the gates were opened the way to them was thronged: an acute ascent—partly rough stairway, partly abrupt incline—which zigzagged up the hill between the wall of the theatre and the wall of an adjacent house and which was lighted, just below its sharpest turn, by a single lamp pendant from an outjutting gib- bet of iron. By a lucky mischance, three of the incompetent officials on duty at the first-class entrance—whereat, in default of guiding

signs, we happened first to apply ourselves—examined in turn our
tickets and assured us that the way to our second-class places was
up that stairway-path. But we heartily forgave, and even blessed,
the stupidity of those officials, because it put us in the way of seeing
quite the most picturesque bit that we saw that night outside of the
theatre's walls: the strong current of eager hu [236] manity, all
vague and confused and sombre, pressing upward through the
shadows, showing for a single moment—the hurrying mass re-
solved into individual hurrying figures—as it passed beneath the
hanging lamp, and in the same breath swept around the projecting
corner and lost to view. It looked, at the very least, treasons, conspiracies, and mutinous outbursts—that shadowy multitude surg-
ing up that narrow and steep and desperately crooked dusky foot-
way. I felt that just around the lighted turn, where the impetuous
forms appeared clearly in the moment of their disappearance, surely must be the royal palace they were bent upon sacking; and it was
with a sigh of unsatisfied longing that I turned away (when we got
at last the right direction) before word came to me that over the
swords of his dying guardsmen they had pressed in and slain the
king!

"IT LOOKED
TREASONS, CONSPIRACIES AND MUTINOUS OUTBURSTS"

The soldiers on guard at the ascent, and thickly posted on the hill-side above the highest tiers, gave colour to my fancy. And, actually, it was as guards against assassins that the soldiers were there. Only a little more than two months had passed since the slay [237] ing of President Carnot at Lyons; and the cautionary measures taken to assure the safety of the three ministers at Orange were all the more rigid because one of them was the minister of justice — of all the government functionaries the most feared and hated by anarchists,

128

because he is most intimately associated with those too rare occasions when anarchist heads are sliced off in poor payment for anarchist crimes. This undercurrent of real tragedy—with its possibility of a crash, followed by a cloud of smoke rising slowly above the wreck of the gaily decorated ministerial box—drew out with a fine intensity the tragedy of the stage: and brought into a curious psychological coalescence the barbarisms of the dawn and of the noontime of our human world.

VI

We came again to the front of the theatre: to an entrance—approached between converging railings, which brought the crowd to an angry focus, and so passed its parts [238] singly between the ticket-takers—leading into what once was the postscenium, and thence across where once was the "court" side of the stage to the tiers of stone seats.

THE GREAT
FAÇADE

However aggravating was this entrance-effect in the matter of
composition, its dramatically graded light-and-shade was masterly.
From the outer obscurity, shot forward as from a catapult by the
pushing crowd, we were projected through a narrow portal into a
dimly lighted passage more or less obstructed by fallen blocks of
stone; and thence onward, suddenly, into the vast interior glaring
with electric lamps: and in the abrupt culmination of light there
flashed up before us the whole of the auditorium — a mountain-side

130

of faces rising tier on tier; a vibrant throng of humanity which seemed to go on and on forever upward, and to be lost at last in the star-depths of the clear dark sky.

Notwithstanding the electric lamps—partly, indeed, because of their violently contrasting streams of strong light and fantastic shadow—the general effect of the auditorium was sombre. The dress of the audience [239] —cloaks and wraps being in general use because of the strong mistral that was blowing—in the main was dark. The few light gowns and the more numerous straw hats stood out as spots of light and only emphasized the dullness of the background. The lines of faces, following the long curving sweep of the tiers, produced something of the effect of a grey-yellow haze floating above the surface of a sable mass; and in certain of the strange sharp combinations of light and shade gave an eerie suggestion of such a bodiless assemblage as might have come together in the time of the Terror at midnight in the Place du Grêve. The single note of strong colour—all the more effective because it was a very trumpet-blast above the drone of bees—was a brilliant splash of red running half-way around the mid-height: the crimson draperies in front of the three tiers set apart for the ministerial party and the Félibres. And for a roof over all was the dark star-set sky: whence the Great Bear gazed wonderingly down upon us with his golden eyes. We were in close touch with the higher regions of the universe. At the very moment when [240] the play was beginning there gleamed across the upper firmament, and thence went radiantly downward across the southern reaches of the heavens, a shooting-star.

Not until we were in our seats—at the side of the building, a dozen tiers above the ground—did we fairly see the stage. In itself, this was almost mean in its simplicity: a bare wooden platform, a trifle over four feet high and about forty by sixty feet square, on which, in the rear, was another platform, about twenty feet square, reached from the lower stage by five steps. The upper level, the stage proper, was for the actors; the lower, for the chorus—which should have been in the orchestra. The whole occupied less than a quarter of the space primitively given to the stage proper alone. Of ordinary theatrical properties there absolutely were none—unless in that category could be placed the plain curtain which hung loosely across the lower half of the jagged gap in the masonry where once the splendid royal portal had been.

But if the stage were mean in itself it was heroic in its surroundings: being flanked by the two castle-like wings abutting upon huge [241] half-ruined archways, and having in its rear the scarred and broken mighty wall—that once was so gloriously magnificent and that now, perhaps, is still more exalted by its tragic grandeur of divine decay. And yet another touch of pathos, in which also was a tender beauty, was supplied by the growth of trees and shrubs along the base of the great wall. Over toward the "garden" exit was a miniature forest of figs and pomegranates, while on the "court" side the drooping branches of a large fig-tree swept the very edge of the stage—a gracious accessory which was improved by arranging a broad parterre of growing flowers and tall green plants upon the stage itself so as to make a very garden there; while, quite a masterstroke, beneath the fig-tree's wide-spreading branches were hidden the exquisitely anachronistic musicians, whose dress and whose instruments alike were at odds with the theatre and with the play.

Two ill-advised electric lamps, shaded from the audience, were set at the outer corners of the stage; but the main illumination was from a row of screened footlights which not [242] only made the whole stage brilliant but cast high upward on the wall in the rear—above the gaping ruined niche where once had stood the statue of a god—a flood of strong yellow light that was reflected strongly from the yellow stone: so making a glowing golden background, whence was projected into the upper darkness of the night a golden haze.

VII

With a nice appreciation of poetic effect, and of rising to strong climax from an opening note struck in a low key, the performance began by the appearance in that heroic setting of a single figure: Mademoiselle Bréval, in flowing white draperies, who sang the "Hymn to Pallas Athene," by Croze, set to music by Saint-Saëns— the composer himself, hidden away with his musicians beneath the branches of the fig-tree, directing the orchestra.

The subduing effect produced by Mademoiselle Bréval's entrance was instantaneous. But a moment before, the audience [243] had been noisily demonstrative. As the ministerial party entered, to the music of the "Marseillaise," everybody had roared; there were more roars when the music changed (as it usually does change in France, nowadays) to the Russian Anthem; there were shouts of welcome to various popular personages—notably, and most deservedly, to M. Jules Claretie, to whom the success of the festival so largely was due; from the tiers where the Parisians were seated came good-humored cries (reviving a legend of the Chat Noir) of "Vive notre oncle!" as the excellent Sarcey found his way to his seat among the Cigaliers; and when the poet Frédéric Mistral entered—tall, stately, magnificent—there broke forth a storm of cheering that was not stilled until the minister (rather taken aback, I fancy, by so warm an outburst of enthusiasm) satisfied the subjects of this uncrowned king by giving him a place of honour in the ministerial box.

And then, suddenly, the shouting ceased, the confusion was quelled, a hush fell upon the multitude, as that single figure in white swept with fluttering draperies across from [244] the rear to the front of the stage, and paused for a moment before she began her invocation to the Grecian goddess: whose altar-fires went out in ancient ages, but who was a living and a glorious reality when the building in which was this echo of her worship came new from the hands of its creators—seventeen hundred years ago. The mistral, just then blowing strongly and steadily, drew down upon the stage and swept back the singer's Grecian draperies in entrancing folds. As she sang, standing in the golden light against the golden back-ground, her supple body was swayed forward eagerly, impetuous-ly; above her head were raised her beautiful bare arms; from her shoulders the loose folds of her mantle floated backward, wing-like—and before us, in the flesh, as in the flesh it was of old before the Grecian sculptors, was the motive of those nobly impulsive, urgent statues of which the immortal type is the Winged Victory.

The theory has been advanced that the great size of the Greek stage, and of the palace in its rear which was its permanent set of scenery, so dwarfed the figures of the actors [245] that buskins and padding were used in order to make the persons of the players more in keeping with their surroundings. With submission, I hold that this theory is arrant nonsense. Even on stilts ten feet high the actors still would have been, in one way, out of proportion with the background. If used at all in tragedy, buskins and pads probably were used to make the heroic characters of the drama literally greater than the other characters.

In point of fact, the majestic height of the scene did not dwarf the human figures sustaining serious parts. The effect was precisely the contrary. Mademoiselle Bréval, standing solitary in that great open space, with the play of golden light upon her, became also heroic. With the characters in "Œdipus" and "Antigone" the result was the same: the sombre grandeur of the tragedies was enlarged by the majesty of the background, and play and players alike were up-raised to a lofty plane of solemn stateliness by the stately reality of those noble walls: which themselves were tragedies, because of the ruin that had come to them with age. [246]

Upon the comedy that so injudiciously was interpolated into the program the effect of the heroic environment was hopelessly belit-tling. M. Arène's "L'Ilote" and M. Ferrier's "Revanche d'Iris" are charming of their kind, and to see them in an ordinary theatre—with those intimate accessories of house life which such sparkling trifles require—would be only a delight. But at Orange their sparkle vanished, and they were jarringly out of place. Even the perfect excellence of the players—and no Grecian actress, I am confident, ever surpassed Mademoiselle Rachel-Boyer in exquisitely finished handling of Grecian draperies—could not save them. Quite as dis-tinctly as each of the tragedies was a success, the little comedies were failures: being overwhelmed utterly by their stately surround-ings, and lost in the melancholy bareness of that great stage. It was all the more, therefore, an interesting study in the psychology of the drama to perceive how the comparatively few actors in the casts of the tragedies—how even, at times, only one or two figures—seemed entirely to fill the stage; and how at [247] all times those plays and their setting absolutely harmonized.

VIII

Of scenery, in the ordinary sense of the word, there was none at all. What we saw was the real thing. In the opening scene of "Œdi-pus," the *King*—coming forward through the royal portal, and across the raised platform in the rear of the stage—did literally "enter from the palace," and did "descend the palace steps" to the "public place" where *Creon* and the priests awaited him. It was a direct reversal of the ordinary effect in the ordinary theatre: where the play loses in realism because a current of necessarily recognized, but purposely ignored, antagonistic fact underruns the conventional illusion and compels us to perceive that the palace is but painted canvas, and (even on the largest stage) is only four or five times as high as the *Prince*. The palace at Orange—towering up as though it would touch the very heavens, and obviously of veritable stone—was a most peremptory reality. [248]

SCENE FROM THE FIRST ACT OF "ŒDIPUS"

The fortuitous accessory of the trees growing close beside the stage added to the outdoor effect still another very vivid touch of realism; and this was heightened by the swaying of the branches, and by the gracious motion of the draperies, under the fitful pressure of the strong gusts of wind. Indeed, the mistral took a very telling part in the performance. Players less perfect in their art would have been disconcerted by it; but these of the Comédie Française were quick to perceive and to utilize its artistic possibilities. In the very midst of the solemn denunciation of *Œdipus* by *Tiresias*, the long white beard of the blind prophet suddenly was blown upward so that his face was hidden and his utterance choked by it; and the momentary pause, while he raised his hand slowly, and slowly freed his face from this chance covering, made a dramatic break in his discourse and added to it a naturalness which vividly intensified its solemn import. In like manner the final entry of *Œdipus*, coming from the palace after blinding himself, was made thrillingly real. For a moment, as he came upon the stage, the hor [249] ror which he had wrought upon himself — his ghastly eye-sockets, his blood-stained face — was visible; and then a gust of wind lifted his mantle and flung it about his head so that all was concealed; and an exquisite pity for him was aroused — while he struggled painfully to rid himself of the encumbrance — by the imposition of that petty annoyance upon his mortal agony of body and of soul.

In such capital instances the mistral became an essential part of the drama; but it was present upon the stage continuously, and its constant play among the draperies — with a resulting swaying of tender lines into a series of enchanting folds, and with a quivering of robes and mantles which gave to the larger motions of the players an undertone of vibrant action — cast over the intrinsic harshness of the tragedy a softening veil of grace.

An enlargement of the same soft influences was due to the entrancing effects of colour and of light. Following the Grecian traditions, the flowing garments of the chorus were in strong yet subdued colour-notes perfectly harmonized. Contrasting with those rich [250] tones, the white-robed figures of the leading characters stood out with a brilliant intensity. And the groups had always a golden background, and over them always the golden glow from the footlights cast a warm radiance that again was strengthened by the golden reflections from the wall of yellow stone, so that the whole symphony in colour had for its under-note a mellow splendour of golden tones.

IX

In this perfect poetic setting the play went on with a stately slowness — that yet was all too fast for the onlookers — and with the perfection of finish that such actors naturally gave to their work amidst surroundings by which they were at once stimulated and inspired. Even the practical defects of the ruinous theatre were turned into poetical advantages which made the tragic action still more real. The woeful entrance of *Œdipus* and the despairing retreat of *Jocasta* were rendered the more impressive by momentary pauses in the broken doorway [251] —that emphasized by its wreck their own wrecked happiness; in "Antigone" a touching beauty was given to the entry of the blind *Tiresias* by his slow approach from the distant side of the theatre, led by a child through the maze of bushes and around the fallen fragments of stone; and Mademoiselle Bartet (*Antigone*), unable to pass by the door that should have been but was not open for her, made a still finer exit by descending the steps at the side of the stage and disappearing among the trees.

But the most perfect of those artistic utilizations of chance accessories—which were the more effective precisely because they were accidental, and the more appreciated because their use so obviously was an inspiration—was the final exit of *Œdipus*: a departure "into desert regions" that Mounet-Sully was able to make very literally real.

Over in the corner beside the "garden" exit, as I have said, was a tangled growth of figs and pomegranates; and thence extending almost to the stage was a light fringe of bushes growing along the base of the rear wall among the fragments of fallen stone. [252] It was through that actual wilderness that *Œdipus*—crossing half the width of the theatre—passed from the brilliant stage into shadow that grew deeper as he advanced, and at last, entering the gap in the stone-work where once the doorway had been, disappeared into the dark depth beyond.

An accident of the moment—the exhaustion of the carbons of the electric lamps—gave to his exit a still keener dramatic intensity. The footlights alone remained burning: flooding with a golden splendour the stage and the great yellow wall, and from the wall reflected upward and outward upon the auditorium; casting over the faces in the orchestra a soft golden twilight, and a still fainter golden light over the more remote hill-side of faces on the tiers—which rose through the golden dusk, and vanished at last in a darkness that still seemed to be a little softened by the faint suggestion of a golden haze.

Interest and light thus together were focused upon the climax of the tragedy. Leaving the light, and with it love and hope and life, behind him, *Œdipus* descended the steps of the palace, leaning upon the shoulder of [253] a slave, and moved toward the thickening shadows. Watching after him with a profoundly sorrowful intensity was the group upon the stage: a gorgeous mass of warm colour, broken by dashes of gleaming white and bathed in a golden glow. Slowly, painfully, along that rough and troublous way, into an ever-deepening obscurity merging into darkness irrevocable, the blinded king went onward toward the outer wilderness where would be spent the dreary remnant of his broken days. Feeling his way through the tangled bushes; stumbling, almost falling, over the blocks of stone; at times halting, and in his desperate sorrow raising his hands imploringly toward the gods whose foreordered curse had fallen upon him because of his foreordered sin, he went on and on: while upon the great auditorium there rested an ardent silence which seemed even to still the beatings of the eight thousand hearts. And when, passing into the black depths of the broken archway, the last faint gleam of his white drapery vanished, and the strain re-laxed which had held the audience still and silent, there came first from all those eager [254] breasts—before the roar of applause which rose and fell, and rose again, and seemed for a while to be quite inextinguishable—a deep-drawn sigh.

X

"Antigone," played on the second evening—being a gentler trag-edy than "Œdipus," and conceived in a spirit more in touch with our modern times—was received with a warmer enthusiasm. No doubt to the Greeks, to whom its religious motive was a living reali-ty, "Œdipus" was purely awe-inspiring; but to us, for whom the religious element practically has no existence, the intrinsic qualities of the plot are so repellent that the play is less awe-inspiring than horrible. And even in Grecian times, I fancy—human nature being the same then as now in its substrata—"Antigone," with its conflict between mortals, must have appealed more searchingly to human hearts than ever "Œdipus" could have appealed with its conflict between a mortal and the gods. Naturally, we are in closer sympa-thy with the righteous [255] defiance of a man by a woman—both before our eyes, passionately flaming with strong antagonistic emo-tions—than we are with a man's unrighteous defiance of abstract and invisible Fate.

138

As "Antigone" was given at Orange, the softening influences which had subdued the harshness of "Œdipus" still farther were extended, making its deep tenderness still deeper and more appealing. The inspersion of music of a curiously penetrating, moving sort—composed by Saint-Saëns in an approximation to Grecian measures—added a poetic undertone to the poetry of the situations and of the lines; and a greater intensity was given to the crises of the play—an artistic reproduction of the effect caused by the accident of the night before—by extinguishing the electric lamps and so bringing the action to a focus in the mellow radiance which came from the golden footlights and richly lighted the stage.

The poetic key-note was struck in the opening scene: when *Antigone* and *Ismene*, robed all in white, entered together by the royal doorway and stood upon the upper plane of [256] the great stage, alone—and yet so filled it that there was no sense of emptiness nor of lack of the ordinary scenery. Again, the setting was not an imitation, but the real thing. The palace from which the sisters had come forth rose stately behind them. Beside the stage, the branches of the fig-tree waved lightly in the breeze. In the golden glow of the footlights and against the golden background the two white-robed figures—their loose vestments, swayed by the wind, falling each moment into fresh lines of loveliness—moved with an exquisite grace. And all this visible beauty reinforced with a moving fervour the penetrating beauty of *Antigone's* avowal of her love for her dead brother—tender, human, natural—and of her purpose, born of that love, so resolute that to accomplish it she would give her life.

SCENE FROM THE SECOND ACT OF "ANTIGONE"

Again, the utter absence of conventional scenery was a benefit rather than a disadvantage. When *Creon* entered upon the upper plane, attended by his gorgeous guard, and at the same moment the entrance of the chorus filled the lower plane with colour less brilliant but not less strong, the stage was full, not of [257] things, but of people, and was wholly alive. The eye was not distracted by painted scenery—in the ordinary theatre a mechanical necessity, and partly excusable because it also supplies warmth and richness of tone—but was entirely at the service of the mind in following the dramatic action of the play. The setting being a reality, there was no need for mechanism to conceal a seamy side; and the colour-effects were produced by the actors themselves: whose draperies made a superb colour-scheme of strong hues perfectly harmonized, of gleaming white, of glittering golden embroideries—which constantly was rearranged by the shifting of the groups and single figures into fresh combinations; to which every puff of wind and every gesture gave fresh effects of light and shade; and over which the golden light shed always its warm radiance.

Of all those beautiful groupings, the one which most completely fulfilled the several requirements of a picture—subject, composition, colour, light-and-shade—was that of the fourth episode: the white-robed *Antigone* alone upon the upper plane, an animate [258] statue, a veritable Galatea; the chorus, a broad sweep of warm colour, on the lower plane; the electric lights turned off, leaving the auditorium in semi-obscurity, and concentrating light and thought upon the golden beauty of the stage. With the entry of *Creon* and his guards both the dramatic and the picturesque demands of the situation were entirely satisfied. In the foreground, a mass of strong subdued colour, were the minor figures of the chorus; in the background, a mass of strong brilliant color, were the minor figures of the guards; between those groups—the subject proper—were *Creon* and *Antigone*: their white robes, flashing with their eager gestures and in vivid relief against the rich background, making them at once the centre and the culmination of the magnificent composition. And the beauty and force of such a setting deepened the pathos and intensified the cruelty of the alternately supplicating and ferocious lines.

There was, I regret to say, an absurd anticlimax to that noble scene. *Antigone*, being recalled and made the centre of a volley of bouquets, ceased to be *Antigone* and became [259] only Mademoiselle Bartet; and the Greek chorus, breaking ranks and scampering about the stage in order to pick up the leading lady's flowers, ceased to be anything serious and became only ridiculous. For the moment French gallantry rose superior to the eternal fitness of things, and in so doing partially destroyed one of the most beautiful effects ever produced upon the stage. Even in the case of minor players so complete a collapse of dignity would not easily have been forgiven. In the case of players so eminent, belonging to the first theatre in the world, it was unpardonable.

XI

But it could be, and was, for the time being forgotten—as the play went on with a smooth perfection, and with a constantly increasing dramatic force, as the action strengthened and quickened in accord always with the requirements of dramatic art.

Without any apparent effort to secure picturesque effect, with a grouping seemingly [260] wholly unstudied and always natural, the stage presented a series of pictures ideal in their balance of mass, and in their colour and tone, while the turning off and on of the electric lights produced effects analogous to those in music when the soft and hard pedals are used to give to the more tender passages an added grace and delicacy, and to the stronger passages a more brilliant force. And always, be it remembered, the play thus presented was one of the most tenderly beautiful tragedies possessed by the world, and the players—by natural fitness and by training—were perfect in their art.

Presently came the end—not a climax of action; not, in one sense, a climax at all. With a master-touch, Sophocles has made the end of "Antigone" the dead after-calm of evil action—a desolate despair. Slowly the group upon the stage melted away. *Creon*, with his hopeless cry upon his lips, "Death! Death! Only death!" moved with a weary languor toward the palace and slowly disappeared in the darkness beyond the ruined portal. There was a pause before the chorus uttered its final solemn words. And then [261] —not as though obeying a stage direction, but rather as though moved severally by the longing in their own breasts to get away from that place of sorrow—those others also departed: going slowly, in little groups and singly, until at last the stage was bare.

The audience was held bound in reality by the spell which had seemed to bind the chorus after *Creon's* exit. Some moments passed before that spell was broken, before the eight thousand hearts beat normally again and the eight thousand throats burst forth into noisy applause—which was less, perhaps, an expression of gratitude for an artistic creation rarely equalled than of the natural rebound of the spirit after so tense a strain. In another moment the seats were emptied and the multitude was flowing down the tiers — a veritable torrent of humanity — into the pit: there to be packed for a while in a solid mass before it could work its way out through the insufficient exits and so return again to our modern world.

And then the Roman Theatre — with a fresh [262] legend of beauty added to the roll of its centuries — was left desert beneath the bright silence of the eternal stars.

Saint-Remy-de-Provence,
December, 1894.

THE END

FOOTNOTES

[1] *Recipe for Poumpo*: Flour, 10½ oz.; brown sugar, 3½ oz.; virgin olive oil (probably butter would answer), 3½ oz.; the white and the yolk of one egg. Knead with enough water to make a firm paste. Fold in three and set to rise for eight or ten hours. Shape for baking, gashing the top. Bake in a slow oven.

[2] *Vin cue*, literally cooked wine, is made at the time of the vintage by the following recipe: Boil unfermented grape-juice in a well scoured cauldron [or porcelain-lined vessel] for a quarter of an hour, skimming thoroughly. Pour into earthen pans, and let it stand until the following day. Pour again into the cauldron, carefully, so as to leave the dregs, and boil until reduced to one-half — or less, or more, according to the sweetness desired. A good rule is to boil in the wine a quince stuck full of cloves — the thorough cooking of the quince shows that the wine is cooked too. Set to cool in earthen pans, and when cold bottle and cork and seal. The Provençal cooked-wine goes back to Roman times. Martial speaks of "Cocta fumis musta Massiliensis."

[3] The admirable edition of Saboly's noëls, text and music, published at Avignon in the year 1856 by François Seguin has been reissued by the same publisher in definitive form. It can be obtained through the Librarie Roumanille, Avignon.

[4] As yet (1902) these high hopes have not been fully realized. In the past eight years dramatic performances repeatedly have been given in the Orange theatre, and always with a brilliant success; but their establishment as fixtures, to come off at regular intervals, still is to be accomplished.

[5] The dimensions of the theatre are: width, 338 feet; depth, 254 feet; height of façade and of rear wall of stage, 120 feet; radius of auditorium, 182 feet.

[6] The conventions of the Greek theatre — and, later, of the Roman theatre — prescribed that through the great central portal kings should enter; through the smaller side portals, queens or princesses (on the left) and guests (on the right); from the portals in the wings, natives of the country (on the left) and strangers (on the right). The

conventional entrances from the wings arose from the fact that the spectators in the Dionysiac theatre, on the Acropolis, saw beyond the stage on the one side the white houses of Athens and on the other the plains of Attica: and so to them the actors coming from the Athenian side were their own people, while those entering from the side toward Attica were strangers. In the modern French theatre the "court" and "garden" entrances still preserve this ancient tradition.